Reach Your Perfect Audience

D1615942

Reach Your Perfect Audience

Leverage the Power of Facebook Advertising to Target Your Ideal Customer

Dave Pittman

Wow Creative Media Publishing

Santa Cruz, CA

First edition: v1.3

First Printing, 2015

Printed in the United States of America

Published by Wow Creative Media, LLC

ISBN: 978-0-9863124-0-3 (digital)

ISBN: 978-0-9863124-1-0 (paperback)

Dedication

For anyone who has a product, a service, a gift, a voice, or a message to share with the world…

May this book provide guidance, insight, and a path to help you reach your perfect audience.

And…

For anyone who feels they have a book inside them but doesn't know how to get it out…

May this serve as an inspiration and example that *you* can do this too!

The world needs to hear your voice, your wisdom, and your experience.

Let it out! And let your light shine.

Table of Contents

Acknowledgements

To Mike Koenigs, for your mentorship, guidance, instruction, and inspiration over these past few years. Thank you! I'm a true believer in your mission.

To Pam Hendrickson, Ed Rush, Paul Colligan, and the rest of the crew at IC/TG. Thank you all for your instruction, guidance, leadership, and being great role models as implementers.

To my AEMM Mastermind colleagues - if it wasn't for co-authoring our book together, this one may never have been birthed. I'm appreciative and grateful for each of you!

To the Publish & Profit, Make Market Launch It, You Everywhere Now, and Instant Customer communities over the years – thank you for your friendship and support!

To my family and friends who have supported me the entire way and have been my biggest cheerleaders — my heartfelt love and thanks!

Preface

Welcome! I am honored that you are here, and feel both grateful and excited that you've taken time out of your busy schedule to read and invest in this book. It's been a labor of love to write and publish it, and I truly hope you find tremendous value in it and learn some game-changing insights as a result.

I say "invest" because time is our most precious commodity, and as business owners in particular, there are so many things competing for our time and attention these days! I get it. So any time you set aside to learn about a new topic, or a new set of strategies and tactics, or some method that can help you grow your business and profits, it truly is an investment.

I also firmly believe that all marketing *should* be an investment! When approached strategically, planned for purposefully, and executed properly, marketing should never be just another cost or expense to your business. Rather, taken as a whole, it should produce a positive return on your investment that not only grows your business, but also allows you to reinvest more money back into your marketing efforts to scale and grow your profits even further. This ROI potential has never been more true in today's marketing environment than with the Facebook platform.

This book is very much about the what and the why, not the how. The "what" because you need to be aware of the most current strategies and capabilities available to you as a business owner on how to get more leads, clients, customers, and grow your business. Whether you are a hands-on do-it-yourself type, have existing staff to implement for you, or you hire outside experts to help, it is always prudent to have a base level of knowledge and common understanding to be able to speak intelligently about the subject or effort at hand. The "why" because you want the confidence and assurance that you are implementing the right strategies for the right reasons that make sense for *your* business, and that you are proceeding thoughtfully and strategically with the solutions proposed here, rather than be distracted by every opportunist or fleeting option thrown your way.

There are a few reasons why we don't dive into the "how." First, if we get into the nitty-gritty details and step-by-step how-to's on every aspect of Facebook advertising, then this book would likely be three times the size, and should be named the "Facebook Advertising Bible." This was neither my intention nor purpose.

Secondly, detailed how-to guides are often best delivered and received in other formats, in the likes of on-line instructional videos, step-by-step workbooks, or course curriculum designed for such purposes. Textbook style how-to's can not only be dry, but somewhat limiting in their effectiveness when it only addresses one form of learning modality, and not easily adaptable as things change.

Third, we all know that the "one constant is change", and that's never been more true in the rapidly changing and evolving world of online social media, internet-based solutions, and technology in general. I purposely minimized the number of screenshots and images of Facebook's various advertising interfaces and tools because they are likely to change and be updated many times in the future. I want the book's subject matter and the strategies and principles discussed to have lasting value, and live beyond the shortened life of how a particular screen or interface looks in the present moment.

Fourth, let's face it — you are a smart and busy individual, and the constraints on your time are probably already great. You can best serve your customers, clients, and patients when you stay in your element: being the professional, expert, and craftsman that you are. As business owners, we often wear too many hats and limit our own effectiveness and growth potential by not staying within our own area of expertise, and trying to do it all. Even if you have a penchant for tech and like to be hands on with everything (I get that too!), sometimes the wisest and most freeing act we can give ourselves as business owners is to focus on what we do best, and let others do the rest. Hand off or hire the "how to" and implementation tasks to other experts, and stay in your own genius zone.

With that said, I don't want to leave you lacking when it comes to implementation and execution. While some tough editorial decisions had to be made on what to include and not include in the book, the best way to continue serving and helping you is to provide a number of free resources that supplement and enhance the book content. Campaign checklists, ad copy and design tips, a frequently updated resources guide, and more can be yours for free by visiting our book bonus page listed at the end of this preface.

As Facebook continues to build out its advertising platform and evolve its capabilities and tools, it's important to stay updated on the latest ad strategies and insights you can use to grow your business. Plus, there will certainly be updates and revisions to this book over time, and I want to make sure you have access to the latest version as they are released. Be sure to connect with me via one of the methods below, so that we can stay in touch and continue the conversation. And if you find any mistakes in this book (which are certain to exist!), whether they are grammatical, spelling, or otherwise, I would be most grateful if you would let me know! Please send the error(s) and their chapter or page references directly to me at dave@perfectaudiencebook.com. Thank you in advance!

Finally, on a personal note, I've had a passion for technology and marketing for my entire adult professional career, and I love helping businesses leverage both of these to their strategic advantage for greater benefit, enjoyment, productivity, profit, and growth. As such, it's difficult at times to restrain myself and stay on topic, because there are so many important areas in setting up and creating an overall marketing strategy and roadmap for your business. To be candid, while Facebook advertising can be a powerful strategic weapon in your marketing arsenal, jumping in directly can be like putting the cart before the horse for some businesses. You want to ensure you have some basic components in place, or at minimum, be in the process of developing them in parallel as you also explore Facebook advertising options. Some of these can include a Facebook Page for your business, another website presence or landing page destination to drive traffic to, a free lead magnet offer to capture leads and build your list, your core product or service offer for sale, and ideally all executed inside a marketing funnel that is automated and systematized.

While beyond the scope of this book, if we can be of any assistance in these areas or with other aspects of your marketing efforts, we offer consulting, done-with-you and full done-for-you services in a number of areas. Please visit www.wowcreativemedia.com to review our services and schedule an initial consultation.

Thanks again for your time, and I hope you receive ten times the value in return. Read it. Learn as you go. Take action. Enjoy the process. And profit!

I wish you the very best of success.

Dave Pittman

Santa Cruz, California, USA

December, 2014

For your free collection of resources to supplement the content of this book, please visit

www.perfectaudiencebook.com/bonus

Or

Text your name and email address to 415-691-BOOK (2665)

Or

Text the word PERFECT to x58885

Or

Scan this QR Code

Part One

Chapter 1

Introduction and Foundation

If you were to ask any business owner what makes their business a *real* business — not just a hobby, or an idea, or a startup with great potential — but an actual living, breathing viable business, what would they say? Is it the tax filing status or incorporation papers that make it official? Is it the service you have to offer, a great product on the shelf, or the merchandise in stock ready for delivery? Is it the backend accounting system installed, the sales staff hired, or the marketing, branding, and logo designed for the company?

What is the one essential component that, without it, would make all the above for naught?

The answer for almost every person, whether instinctively or upon careful reflection is *customers*.

It's universal. **Customers are the lifeblood of any business**. The operations of a business consist of many functions and moving parts, but ultimately without customers, you don't have a real business; or rather, a business that's going to last.

As a business owner, and in particular if you are a small business owner, solo-professional ("solopreneur"), or entrepreneur, you likely wear many hats and juggle multiple priorities and tasks at any given time. Involved in every aspect of running your business, day-to-day operations or pressing matters often compete with your time spent on delivering your actual products or services and focusing on what matters most: creating happy satisfied customers, clients, and patients that will keep returning for more of what you have to offer, and then ensuring that a steady flow of new prospects and customers continue to come your way.

As a service professional, private practice professional, or a practitioner of a trade who has spent years in apprenticeship, school, ongoing study and perfecting your craft, learning how to "run a business" is often a secondary, on-the-job training process and trial by fire. "Sales" is considered a dirty word and necessary evil, and marketing is often an afterthought or another expense, thrown onto the "I'll get to it one day" pile.

Yet marketing is the very initiator and source, the spark plug and wellspring of that lifeblood of customers we all agree is so crucial. While a variety of challenges and opportunities face every business, the one consistent (and often biggest) challenge mentioned time and time again in surveys, studies, and in our own consultation is, "How do I get more traffic, leads, prospects, and customers to grow my business?"

Imagine now for a moment that we can wave a magic wand and solve this biggest challenge. A steady stream of new traffic and leads is now flowing into your business. What could possibly be better than this scenario? How about not having just *any* traffic and leads come your way, but attracting only the *right* leads and customers in the first place! Those customers who are already aligned with your business, love what you have to offer, and continue to buy from you again and again. Your ideal clients who actually follow your advice, get results, and become your biggest fans, loyal supporters, and best source of referrals -- customers and clients for life.

If marketing is the path to generating new leads and customers in general, then the *right* type of targeted, focused marketing is the golden key to getting those ideal leads and customers for your business.

Traditional forms of marketing and advertising generally focus on reaching the masses, casting a wide net into the vast ocean in hopes that the specific fish they want will get caught in the process. Think about it: the success of traditional advertising like print and newspaper ads, radio spots, and TV commercials all depend on your target customer listening to the exact radio station and time of day that your spot airs, or be watching on the exact TV channel during the time your commercial shows (and with on-demand streaming and DVRs these days, who watches commercials anymore?), or flipping through the very pages of the newspaper section where your print ad appears. Not only are you largely relying on hope or chance, but you're paying a lot of money for exposure to people who have no interest in your products or services in the first place, and that can be very costly. There must be a better way!

Today's Marketing Environment

The previous paragraph was not intended to completely dismiss traditional forms of advertising, as these approaches have successfully worked for decades, and still can with the right objectives and expectations. But with the advent of the internet and today's modern technologies, the marketing landscape has radically changed in terms of cost effective solutions (as traditional advertising can still be prohibitively expense), the ability to measure and track performance in ways not possible before, and the ability to target your market based on detailed data previously unimaginable.

There is a well-known formula in marketing known as the three M's: target the right Market with the right Message via the right Media (or Medium). All three M's are important to succeed, but too often the initial and sometimes sole focus is placed on the more tactical portion of the trio: media — producing marketing brochures, collateral, and other print material for handouts, advertisements, etc. Little, if any attention is given to really identifying your core market and truly understanding your ideal customer at a deep level first, and then correspondingly tailor the right message to that market segment, known as "message to market match."

This book focuses on the first and arguably most important M of the trifecta — market — through the lens of the third M: one of the most powerful media platforms for *targeting* that market — Facebook. Facebook is the golden key spoken about above that helps you reach your perfect audience and target your ideal customer.

Facebook

There is no question that Facebook plays a unique role in the ever-connected world that we live in, and has firmly cemented itself in a prominent place within the annals of Internet history. From its humble beginnings in a dorm room at Harvard, to its storied rise and rapid growth up to our present time, Facebook has become the largest, most dominant social networking platform online today.

If you are among the one-fifth of the world's population who uses Facebook on a monthly basis, then you need no introduction to how it has shaped the way we share, engage, communicate, and stay connected with our family and friends, irrespective of time zone, location, or distance. There is no question that Facebook is here to stay for the long haul, and if you haven't done so already, it's time to seriously consider what role it can and <u>should</u> play in your business and marketing strategy.

Purpose of this Book

Much has been written already about social media marketing, including many books dedicated to specific platforms like Facebook. This is not a general-purpose overview on Facebook marketing, nor is it intended to be a complete A to Z reference guide on Facebook advertising. **My goal is really to help you, the reader, get more of that lifeblood flow of new customers into your business, utilizing one of the most powerful platforms in existence today.** If set up strategically and executed properly, you can literally have successful advertising campaigns running like faucets: turn on when you need a new flow of clients and patients; turn off when you've had your fill (until you're ready for more and turn on again). Or, depending on the nature of your business, have it running full time for a steady stream of new prospects and customers. Most importantly, not just any customers, but the *right* ones for your business. If this sounds good to you, then you are in the right place!

With this purpose and goal in mind, our focus in this book is on three primary objectives:

1. Make the case for paid advertising in today's marketing environment, and explain why relying on free traffic alone is neither sufficient nor effective if you want to maximize your results in a short amount of time

2. Answer the question "Why Facebook?" as an advertising platform, and why you can no longer afford to ignore it, no matter what business you're in

3. Dive deep into what truly sets Facebook apart — audience targeting — and how you can use this to define your ideal market, tailor your message, and harness Facebook's power to grow your customers, sales, and profits

This last objective is where we spend the bulk of our time together. I provide a thorough review of all the ways you can identify and select your target audience within Facebook, so that you are armed and educated with the knowledge of what's possible, and can begin using this to create your own advertising campaigns.

With these objectives stated, here's what I hope you, the reader, will take away from this book:

• Be fully educated on the power of Facebook advertising and how to leverage its targeting capabilities to reach your perfect audience

- Be inspired and excited about the possibilities this offers you to
    - Expand your reach and visibility
    - Get more of your ideal fans, followers, leads, clients, and customers
    - Grow your sales, profits, and business
    - Advertise in an affordable, cost-effective way with positive ROI (where your profits exceed your costs, essentially making it free to advertise!)
- Be compelled to use Facebook ads as part of your marketing strategy. Make it a "no brainer" and a must-do
- Be encouraged to take action NOW. There is no better time!

I truly believe you will be amazed at the richness of data and level of granularity available in Facebook to identify, target, and reach your perfect audience (hence, the title of this book!), and by the time you finish reading, I trust you will be both excited and full of ideas on how you can apply this for your business.

Who This Is For

In keeping with our theme, let me share who my "perfect audience" is for this book. With a sense of irony I acknowledge my answer doesn't align with some primary advice given throughout this book, which is to get specific, selective, and focused when defining your target market. The simple reality is, with over a billion people on Facebook from around the world, *anyone* who is seeking to reach an audience, for practically any purpose, can benefit from the knowledge and strategies shared here. The only other criterion is a willingness to invest in paid advertising to reach them. And if you aren't convinced of this yet, you will be after reading this book! So the "on the fencers" are welcome here too.

With that said, we started this chapter discussing the importance of customers and how vital they are to any business. Thus, business owners have the most to gain here, and yet there are hardly any restrictions on what type of business, profession, trade, or form your business takes. Beneficiaries of this knowledge are many, whether you are an

- Entrepreneur or business owner of any type, practice, industry or size (online or offline, B2B or B2C)
- Author, speaker, coach, consultant, or professional of any kind
- Information marketer, online marketer, or network marketer
- Blogger, hobbyist, artist, creative type or individual with a passion, voice, or message to share

Let me address this last group specifically in case you don't have a "business" per se. The beauty and power of the Facebook platform is both its massive reach as well as its incredible targeting capabilities to narrow down that reach to any desirable size based on a variety of different criteria. The key here is that your audience can comprise of whatever and whomever you want them to be, whether they are leads, prospects and customers (i.e. business-oriented), or simply readers, fans, followers, enthusiasts, donators, activists, consumers, tribe members or fellow _____ (fill in the blank, whoever that is for *you*).

So whether you have a product, a service, a cause, or simply a message you want to share with the entire world, or only to the smallest and narrowest of niches — in other words, *YOUR perfect audience* — then **there is no better platform right now than Facebook to get your message out there, and to use paid advertising as the medium to accelerate and maximize your reach to that market.**

But My Business is Different...

While we covered virtually all our bases above in terms of who can benefit, let me address the elephant in the room that occasionally shows up when someone questions whether a new marketing channel or set of strategies like we'll cover is applicable to their business. Or as my mentor Mike Koenigs calls it, the "Yeah-but" monster. "*Yeah, but* my business is different", or "*Yeah, but* this wouldn't work in my industry", or "*Yeah, but* my customers aren't on Facebook", or "*Yeah, but* my business is offline only". Let's slay this monster right now and state that when it comes to proven, time-tested strategies and principles that pertain to marketing, lead generation and sales, they can be adapted and applied to virtually any type of business. It's a myth and mental trap that business owners too often fall into when something new doesn't initially work out, or a half-hearted attempt results in failure (with no real strategy or proper execution plan followed), or worse — no action is taken at all. They fall back on the excuse that "this won't work for me" or "I don't have the time or budget" to justify their current state.

So let's address some doubts as they pertain specifically to Facebook.

First, before you assume your target audience or clientele isn't on Facebook, please suspend judgment until you've read the rest of this book. There's a very strong chance that they are and you just don't know it yet. And yes, if you are wondering specifically about this — Facebook works for B2B companies too!

Second, even if your business is largely or 100% offline, I can guarantee you that your customers aren't! A now famous study done by BIA/Kelsey showed that 97% of all consumers use some form of online media when researching products or services in their local area. Ninety Seven Percent! This has huge implications for local businesses. And here's the kicker — that study was done back in 2010, almost 5 years ago now!

You may *think* your business is offline, but I guarantee your current and future customers are looking for you *and* likely talking about you online, via social media, review sites, business directories, and other channels. If you are not actively participating in the conversation — connecting, engaging, influencing, and managing your reputation, or simply letting them know you exist with some minimum form of online presence — then you are effectively relinquishing control of your own message, marketing, and brand to the public. Ignorance is not bliss in this situation, and what you don't know *can* hurt you in the long run. If you find yourself in this state and need to re-think your online marketing strategy (or develop one if you have no presence online at all), this may be your most important takeaway from the entire book. (If you are just getting started building your online presence and platform, please check the back of the book for resources that may help you.)

Third, some of the best marketing ideas can come from studying what others are doing *outside* of your current industry or profession, and applying those approaches in your own business. This is how marketing legend (and another mentor) Jay Abraham has literally made billions for his clients over the last 40 years. If you ever find yourself saying "Everyone in my line of business does it this way, so I assume that's what I should do too", then pause and reflect. *Maybe* that will work if they are actually producing good results. Or, perhaps that's the very reason why they all find themselves in the same slump — following the herd and each other like blind mice, and then scratching their heads wondering why things aren't working.

Now, imagine you "borrow" a marketing approach or idea from another industry and apply it to your own. Bam! This could be the very spark that jumpstarts your growth, reignites your business, and gets you moving again well past your competition. *Now* if you catch yourself thinking, "But my profession or industry doesn't advertise on Facebook..." did some new light bulbs go off?! Facebook could be the very answer you've been seeking that causes your next level breakthrough in acquiring new leads, clients and customers. I've seen it work time and time again in businesses of all sizes, and I'm confident it can work for your business too.

What's Ahead

Here's what you can look forward to in the chapters ahead. First, we explain why paid advertising is the fastest, most effective way to get your product, service or message in front of your target audience. Free traffic is nice and welcomed, but you can't build a serious business relying on something that can be fickle, unpredictable, and takes a while before seeing fruitful results.

Next, we explain why Facebook is the most powerful platform in today's marketing environment to use for your advertising strategy, and lay out the numbers to prove it. We then provide a quick high-level overview of the Facebook ads environment, where we cover some key concepts and terminology that is used throughout the remainder of the book.

In section two, we jump into the powerful audience selection and targeting capabilities that sets Facebook apart from all other advertising platforms. Multiple chapters are devoted to in-depth descriptions of the different selection criteria available to define your audience, including: location, demographics, interests, behaviors, and connections.

We then dive into three advanced targeting capabilities that take your reach to a whole new level. The first two are Custom Audiences and Website Custom Audiences that let you target people on Facebook whom you already have a relationship with elsewhere, via your email lists, offline customer lists, or visitors to your website. Then, Lookalike Audiences allow you to expand your reach and target those who have affinity with your existing audience, lists, or customers, based on similar demographics, interests, and behaviors. It's a powerful way to greatly expand your reach to more people who are just like the existing customers you already have, and thus have a greater propensity to like you and buy from you.

We then wrap up with some fantastic tips and guidance on how to conduct more advanced market research to dig even deeper and gain greater insights into your target audience, using both external resources and some powerful tools within Facebook itself.

So get comfortable, grab your favorite beverage, be prepared to take lots of notes, and get ready to learn all about the power of Facebook advertising.

Chapter 2

The Case for Paid Advertising

Free.

Who doesn't like the sound of that? When it comes to your online presence or business, receiving free spoils from the web is generally welcomed — free traffic, visitors, clicks, likes, shares, retweets, and reposts; free (positive) press, publicity, PR, and media exposure which ideally lead to free customers, clients, and patients; and free referrals and recommendations that turn into more free traffic, leads, prospects and customers in an never-ending cycle. Ah, if it were only that easy. Life would be good, and your online business would be one continuous source of cash flow, profits, and bliss.

But is free all that it's cracked up to be? And does "free" ever *truly* mean free? Since the beginnings of the Internet, there have always been golden windows of opportunity with the advent and arrival of some new technology, platform, tool, or communication channel, in which there was a distinct first-mover advantage. Those who were early adopters of said platform, media, or tool often reaped huge benefits over those who were ignorant of its arrival, played a "wait and see" approach, or who were just late to the table after mass adoption had already occurred. In the context of the web, these benefits often meant free and easy traffic, visitors, visibility, exposure, and reach.

Search traffic

For example, if you had an online presence during the earliest days of the world wide web, a few basic search engine optimization (SEO) tweaks was all it took to rank your website on page one of the search engines, as most people knew little, if anything, about this topic. As the number of websites exploded over many years and Google rose in popularity, more attention to SEO fundamentals and strategies became the norm for website developers, along with various ways and attempts to hack and exploit the system to unfairly boost rankings. Google would then respond by changing its search algorithm, effectively negating all the "tricks" that people deployed to game the system, and reward those website owners who played by the rules.

As further exploits became even more elaborate and sophisticated, Google would continue responding with more changes to the inner workings of its search engine, to effectively shut down any nefarious attempts at gaming the system. In the industry, these questionable tactics and exploits become known as "black hat" SEO (vs. "white hat" SEO which is compliant, play-by-the-rules SEO, and "gray hat" which is somewhere in-between), and this inevitable cat-and-mouse game continues to this day.

Why go to such great lengths to rank high in Google? While the answer is probably obvious, appearing above the fold (top visible area of a page without needing to scroll down) on Google's search engine results page for your keywords is arguably the most coveted real estate on the web. Statistics continuously show that the farther down the page your link appears, the number of clicks drop significantly, with an even more dramatic drop-off on page two and beyond. With over 40,000 searches per *second* and 3.5 billion searches per day, ranking high in organic (non-paid) search results is all about achieving one thing — free traffic.

Free?

The irony, of course, is that it is usually anything but free. Any serious Ecommerce business or other website that depends heavily on high ranking organic search results are likely paying hundreds, if not thousands of dollars per month on SEO expertise to continuously build, maintain, and improve their rankings.

Is it really free when you are constantly paying experts to help you manage your search results? Is it really free when you are expending your valuable time, energy, and effort (or those of your staff) to do this yourself or in house? And is it really free when one of the "experts" you hire either knowingly or unknowingly deploys a questionable SEO tactic that may get you great results at first, only to wake up one morning and discover your website has suddenly disappeared off the face of planet Google?

Sadly, many online businesses have shutdown within days (in some cases, literally overnight) after a major search engine update has been released, effectively being penalized and banned for not playing by the rules and going outside the boundaries of acceptable practices. You (or the hired expert) may think you can outsmart the proverbial 800-pound gorilla in the short term with some traffic-getting hack, but it's only a matter of time before Google's well-staffed and well-paid army of exceptionally bright engineers crack down on your exploits to keep the playing field level and fair for all "law abiding" netizens.

SEO

Let me be clear that this illustration is not intended to dismiss the importance of SEO by any means. Applying SEO fundamentals and best practices to your website and other online properties is an important part of any sound marketing strategy, with the realization that this is a longer term play.

Even if you are completely compliant and apply all the right tactics when it comes to SEO, it can sometimes take many months or years to build up your organic page ranking and SERP (search engine results page) position, especially if you are in a competitive space or your website is relatively new. And if you are a smaller operation up against some well-financed big competitors, they can likely outspend you month after month to stay on top.

Or, if you enjoy a strong page one ranking now, sometimes there is a reluctance to make any significant changes or updates to your website in fear of somehow "messing up" its optimization and thus lose your positioning (the "don't touch it!" syndrome, at the expense of your website showing its age and looking out of date).

The reality is that Google will invariably continue to modify its algorithm over time in response to the ever-changing nature of the web and the evolution of search itself. Thus, this is one area where the learning curve remains ongoing, and occasional adjustments to one's search optimization strategies are part of the norm. This may frustrate some website owners (although it really shouldn't if you avoid the schemes and gimmicks, and just focus on adding great value and content for your audience), but it sure keeps the SEO experts happy and their agencies in business!

Website First, Social Second

While we just spent a significant amount of time discussing search, this is a relevant topic to cover in this context, as it is the default starting point for finding things online and, on the recipient side, to getting discovered and found. And by default, it's free to use for both purposes.

Additionally, my assumption is that you already have a business website in place as your "home base" on the web, even as you build out and expand your online presence in other areas. It is never wise to build your entire online strategy solely and exclusively around a single social media platform (even Facebook), because you are ultimately not in control when you play in someone else's playground. Those who own the platform get to make the rules, which can change at any time (just like the search engines)! What's super hot today may evolve significantly over time, or not even be around in a few years from now (can anyone say MySpace?).

While the entire next chapter is devoted to making a strong case for Facebook's relevance, longevity, and staying power, you should never put all your eggs in one basket. Furthermore, everything you will learn in this book about the power of Facebook advertising ultimately drives your audience back to somewhere else to learn more about you and ultimately buy your products and services, which typically is your website. Takeaway lesson: If you do not yet have a website for your business that you have complete control over, please make this a top priority.

Early Adopter benefits

To return back to our original premise at the outset of this chapter, those with an early online web presence or who adopted SEO principles early in the game were rewarded with free traffic, visibility and exposure. These rewards held true for many other technologies and platforms when they first came into being as well. Early users of video on the web (for both personal and business) have seen huge benefits in terms of visibility and free traffic. To this day, video is still one of the best ways to rank high in search results if done well and optimized appropriately, and any business that utilizes video on their website or has an active YouTube channel will have a marked advantage over their competition.

All the major social media platforms of the last few years, whether it's Twitter, LinkedIn, Pinterest, Instagram, YouTube, or Facebook, provided direct and indirect benefits for those who jumped on board early. Considering Facebook is the largest social network of them all and our book's focus, let's briefly review the benefits of its early years and the new realities of today from a business perspective.

Facebook Pages - "The Early Years"

To quickly ensure we are all speaking the same language and have a common understanding of Facebook's terminology, let's clarify a couple terms that are often used interchangeably but mean different things. Every individual user of Facebook has a personal *profile*, but a business, organization, or brand on Facebook have pages (often called "fan pages"). It's not uncommon for people to also refer to their profile as their "page", but in the context of this book, and in official Facebook terms, a page is meant for business or commercial use. (If you are positioning yourself as a brand, personality, or in any professional or business capacity, it is best to create a separate page for yourself. Facebook states that personal profiles should be for non-commercial use only.)

Facebook pages were first announced in 2007 as part of the introduction of Facebook Ads, and were designed to allow businesses to connect and interact with their audiences, and vice versa - allowing users to interact and affiliate with businesses in the same way they interact with their friends: commenting, liking, sharing, posting, providing reviews, uploading photos, etc. It is, still to this day, one of the most powerful and unique features of Facebook's platform — the ability for brands and their audiences, fans, and consumers to socially interact and engage with each other, and for a brand's message to be distributed further throughout the social graph, as users communicate and share a company or brand's posts within their own network.

As founder of Facebook, Mark Zuckerberg, states,

> *"Social actions are powerful because they act as trusted referrals and reinforce the fact that people influence people. It's no longer just about messages that are broadcasted out by companies, but increasingly about information that is shared between friends."[1]*

It's as brilliant as it is powerful. What would have more influence on you and build trust: a traditional advertisement randomly displayed online or seen in print, or your friends' personal recommendations and positive comments about that same brand or company? There's no question it's the latter, and numerous consumer research studies prove this over and over again, year after year.

Of course, companies love this! Who wouldn't want an army of fans and followers who genuinely like a product or service you offer, and then turn around and freely act as brand ambassadors as they share that love and passion with their friends, who in turn may recommend it to their own friends, and friends of friends, and so on! Of course, it can work in the opposite direction too (and be far more damaging). Bad news can spread quickly like wildfire, and there are enough infamous stories in recent years where a bad customer experience gone viral on social media can turn into a public relations nightmare. In any case, the power of social is unquestionable, and has forever changed the landscape of B2C (business to consumer) interaction.

How much did businesses jump on this bandwagon? Over 100,000 pages were initially launched on the first day of the big announcement in 2007. Over seven years later, Facebook reports that over 30 million active small & medium business (SMB) pages now exist on the platform today.[2] That's stupendous growth and adoption! And with good reason. Just like the early days of the other platform rollouts, businesses now had a brand new channel to reach consumers directly, and in a way that was unique and revolutionary.

Best of all, it was free! You didn't have to necessarily advertise or spend money, because your business page looked and worked just like a personal profile, and you could literally interact with your followers and fans as if they were friends. Those businesses that "got" what Facebook is all about — that is to say, it's first and foremost a *social* network and not a place to simply pitch, advertise and be "salesy" — likely succeeded. Those businesses that didn't respect the platform or its users and simply promoted all day long like another advertising channel, didn't do as well or worse — suffered negative consequences from consumer backlash, complaints, and poor publicity.

Of course, a lot has happened and evolved over these past seven years! Not only did the number of business pages grow, Facebook's user base exploded as well. At the end of 2007, there were 58 million users; today, over 1.3 billion actively use Facebook every month. And with this explosion in user and page growth comes an even larger exponential growth in content and items that are posted and shared. So much so that it is literally impossible for the system to display every posting made by your friends or the pages you follow, and as a result, there's a lot more competition in the News Feed vying for your attention. Facebook states,

> *"There is now far more content being made than there is time to absorb it. On average, there are 1,500 stories that could appear in a person's News Feed each time they log onto Facebook. For people with lots of friends and Page likes, as many as 15,000 potential stories could appear any time they log on."* [3]

Fifteen hundred stories, let alone fifteen thousand? And you thought your email inbox was out of control! So how does Facebook determine what content to display in your News Feed? Just like Google's "top secret" algorithm that determines how it calculates search rankings for the 30 trillion web pages in its index, Facebook has it own secret recipe, designed to look at thousands of different factors to prioritize and decide which content is most relevant to you.

Originally known as EdgeRank (the name has since been abandoned), there were three primary factors publicly revealed— affinity, weight, and decay — that largely determined what content appeared in your News Feed. While these three are still important, the algorithm has since become even more complex and sophisticated in the last two years, now taking into account literally thousands of different facets and data points, many of which factor in user-driven signals based on actions you've taken on the site.

While Facebook continuously works to improve the algorithm and make updates as necessary, their end goal with News Feed has largely remained the same. In their words, "deliver the right content to the right people at the right time so they don't miss the stories that are important to them."

To complete the punch line — of the 1500 potential stories Facebook can show you at any given time? Only about 20%, or approximately 300 will make it into your News Feed. Welcome to today's reality.

Organic Reach Declining

If you've managed a page for a long time and reminisce about the good old days when your content was widely seen by all, or perhaps you have noticed a steady decline or even a significant drop in your organic reach in the last few months, you are not alone. Many businesses and page owners have voiced their frustrations and concern over this trend, and a study released in early 2014 by Social@Ogilvy showed an almost 50% drop in organic reach for 106 global brand pages they monitored, from 12.05% down to 6.15% within four months. [4]

As illustrated above however, there are two primary reasons for this, the first of which is simple math. More and more content is being created and shared every single day, and is increasing at a faster rate than our ability to consume it. Secondly, and as a result, the News Feed is designed to systematically identify and rank this content to show only what's most relevant to you.

It's often asked why Facebook doesn't provide a real-time chronological feed of every single post. In several tests Facebook have conducted, results show that this not only lowers engagement, but causes too much valuable content to be missed simply because it's not near the top of the News Feed when a person logs in. This decreased organic reach as well.

While it's understandable to lament the loss of organic reach and free visibility with your fans and followers, all of these changes are actually positive signs under fair consideration. First, increases in user growth, content growth, and engagement growth all validate that the platform continues to be strong, viable and healthy. And, it is in Facebook's own best interest to keep its users on their platform for as long as possible, which means they are continuously striving to provide the best user experience it can.

Happy engaged users are not only good for Facebook, but for businesses *on* Facebook. And as they further refine and tweak their algorithms to reduce News Feed spam and show higher-quality content that's interesting, timely, relevant and engaging for its users, the more everyone benefits. In short, these are good things on the whole, and should be great for businesses too!

Facebook Marketing (in a nutshell)

Volumes have been written, both online and in book form, on the subjects of social media marketing in general, and Facebook marketing specifically. While much of it is mediocre at best or a rehashing of the same old (and often outdated) advice over and over, there are a number of really smart marketers and true experts in the field who know, live, and breathe these topics intimately, and most importantly, can back up their claims with testing, data, and results. While many offer specific strategies, tactics, and tips on how to craft posts, when are the best times to post, how to grow your fan base, get more likes, increase engagement, etc., they are all based on some core principles that are foundational to anyone's success on Facebook, no matter the advice.

Let me save you many hours of time, study, and money by summarizing what these fundamentals are that underlie any advice out there that happens to work. I can confidently tell you these are true because they come directly from Facebook themselves. [5] They are:

1) Make your posts timely and relevant
2) Build credibility and trust with your audience
3) Ask yourself, "Would people share this with their friends or recommend it to others?"
4) Think about, "Would my audience want to see this in their News Feeds?"

In a nutshell, focus on high quality content (that's timely, relevant, interesting, and adds value) and optimize it for engagement and reach. Don't spam them with endless promotions, and seek to understand what works best for your particular audience. Finally, remember to keep the "social" in your social network interactions; don't think of Facebook as simply another advertising or marketing channel to take advantage of. If you don't respect the purpose of the platform and why people like to spend time there, you risk damaging your brand, your business, and the relationships with your audience, prospects, and customers.

By all means, follow your favorite experts and gurus who expand upon these and turn them into practical tactics and tips for execution. But if you let these principles guide you in all that you do on Facebook, you will succeed. I mention these here because they will not only help you with your organic reach, but will equally apply when you create your ad content and step into the world of paid media. Let's discuss this next.

Pay to Play

With organic reach down, more competition in the News Feed, and more difficulty to gain exposure, what is a business to do? Facebook's growth and maturation as a platform in many ways parallels the path of the search engines we discussed earlier, with similar impact on those who use them. You can take many months to try and rank organically on page one of Google, or you can cut to the chase and pay for that privilege via Google AdWords.

Similarly, using paid advertising on Facebook will allow you to reach your fans, followers, and customers more predictably, and with greater accuracy than relying on regular posts alone. Additionally, it helps you greatly broaden and expand your audience, reaching out to new prospects and potential customers with targeting capabilities unmatched anywhere else. And when your ads are driven by specific objectives (e.g. like a page, download an app, visit a website, etc., which the system requires you to define), you'll see more effective results that return greater value and ROI to your business.

Bottom line? In today's marketing environment, you must "pay to play."

Your Call to Action

We mentioned above that over 30 million small & medium business pages exist on Facebook today. Of these, only 1.5 million are actively advertising. This is both good news and a call to action. If your business currently isn't on Facebook yet, or your page(s) have been in a dormant or "ignored" state for some time, or you are frustrated with your results and not seeing the level of engagement and reach you want, I encourage you to start now or start fresh again with a renewed sense of purpose and excitement!

There is no better time to leverage Facebook's platform to grow your business, and there is no doubt that paid media is still the fastest and most efficient way to put yourself, your products or services in front of an audience. And with the small ratio of those who currently advertise to total business pages, this is a prime opportunity to position yourself ahead of your competition and reach your market more quickly and effectively.

Your time is now. And it has never looked better!

Chapter 3

Why Facebook

In the previous chapter we spoke to the realities of today's marketing environment, and with the rapid maturity of the various search and social media platforms, made a strong case for paid advertising as a whole. We also laid the groundwork and began looking at why Facebook is such a powerful platform to use as an advertising channel. We'll continue this discussion and start with some impressive statistics announced during their most recent Quarterly Earnings release. [6]

Facebook's massive reach has been mentioned many times. Just how big is it? They now have over 1.35 billion monthly active users which, to put in perspective, is about 20% of the entire human population. If Facebook were a country, it's pretty much on par with China to be the most populous on earth, and will likely overtake them soon. This clearly makes it the largest social media platform to date, far surpassing any other social networks like LinkedIn, Twitter, or Google Plus. While its size is massive, this alone doesn't necessarily make it unique. Google, as a search engine, and its sister property YouTube (If you didn't know, Google owns YouTube) each have over 1 billion unique monthly users respectively.

What *does* make Facebook stand out is how active and engaged its audience is: 864 million users visit **every single day**. In the US alone, Americans spend an average of 40 minutes per day on Facebook [7], and when you look at the total hours spent per person per month, Facebook clocks in at 6 hours, 35 minutes! This is almost double the time spent on Google (3 hours, 20 minutes) and over 300% longer than any Yahoo or Microsoft properties. [8] And these figures only represent desktop usage, not including time spent on mobile smartphones or tablets! Given these are only averages, you probably know family or friends who spend many times this amount on Facebook, perhaps even you?

Next, let's look at mobile — over 1.12 Billion monthly mobile users, of which 703 million log in daily. Of these daily users, 536 million are exclusively mobile. In other words, over 75% of all daily Facebook users *only* log in from a smartphone or tablet. In terms of overall time spent on Facebook across all platforms and devices, 68% is on mobile. These are not just interesting statistics, but another differentiator when it comes to advertising. Facebook allows you to place your ads exclusively on mobile devices if desired (vs. on desktops or both), which further allows you to tailor your ad design and copy specifically for your mobile audience. For example, if you were a mobile app developer or sold mobile accessories like phone cases, headphones, tablet stands, etc., this could be an excellent way to refine your target audience when placing ads.

In summary, with an average of over 4.5 billion daily likes, 4.8 billion daily shares, and 12 billion messages sent every single day by one fifth of the world's population, Facebook gives you the power to connect with, engage, and influence your customers and reach more people, on more devices, in more places than anywhere else. Now that's impressive!

Facebook Targeting

But what if your audience isn't "the world", and you are not a billion-dollar global brand trying to reach the masses? Perhaps you are a hobbyist, blogger, or solopreneur with an online business in a specific niche; an entrepreneur, coach, or consultant serving a particular industry; a service or health professional trying to target your ideal clientele; or a small business owner of a brick-and-mortar shop trying to expand your reach to more people within their neighborhood or city. This is where Facebook really begins to shine.

Facebook comes with an incredibly powerful set of targeting capabilities that are unmatched by any other advertising platform. It can use the profile information and demographics of every user on its network, along with their behaviors, interests, actions, and activities taken throughout the site (and as we'll see later, even their activities *off* site).

Think for a moment about your own personal use of Facebook and what information you share publicly or privately with friends. Now think about all the pages you've liked, the comments you've made, the groups you've joined, the posts you've shared, the places you've checked into, the links you've clicked, the events you've attended, the apps you've downloaded, the stories you've read, or the videos you've watched over time — and then multiply that by over one billion people! All of this builds a rich tapestry of data that not only can advertisers tap into to place relevant and tailored ads before you, but *you,* the business owner, can leverage this very same information to create highly selective and targeted campaigns, customizing ads to specific segments of your market, and ultimately reaching your perfect audience.

Even more, when you ad appears in a person's News Feed, it should not only be designed to look like a normal post (utilizing images, video, links, and text as appropriate) and thus blend in with other activity, but your ad can be liked, commented on, and shared! You gain the benefit of social proof (which strengthens trust, credibility, and increases sales) *and* the ability for your ad to reach even more people through the engagement actions of your audience. Simply put, people make your ads more effective, and the social context of likes and shares signal a positive quality of the ad, which even leads to better and more efficient auction prices. These are powerful benefits not available on any other advertising platform.

Finally, let's briefly talk about the advertising landscape on Facebook. With over $3.2 billion in advertising revenue in its most recent quarter, which is a 59% increase from a year ago, Facebook is in a strong second position behind Google in worldwide ad revenue, and far ahead of any other competitors. It is not our intention in this chapter to provide a detailed Google vs. Facebook comparison or breakdown. In reality, both platforms provide unique advertising advantages and in many cases, it may be appropriate for a business to pursue both.

There are, however, many data points in Facebook's favor that are worth highlighting. In general, Facebook CPC (cost per click) ads are cheaper than Google CPC ads. Facebook has a 35% lower cost per conversion than the online average, and in a recent analysis of over 60 campaigns, 70% of companies had a return of 300% or more on ad spend, and 49% had a 500% or greater ROI (Return on Investment)![9] And according to Nielsen, most online advertising reaches only 38% of its intended audience, whereas Facebook's average is a whopping 89%.[10]

In summary, Facebook has the massive reach, unparalleled targeting capabilities, socially endorsable ads, complete mobile and cross-platform integration, is affordable to get started, and has a consistently higher return on ad spend. It has the power to connect, engage, influence, and drive business results. What's not to like?

Chapter 4

Facebook Ads Overview

Before we dive deep into the subject of audience targeting which is the core focus and next section of this book, I want to provide a brief overview of the Facebook Advertising platform to establish a base level understanding about the different ad objectives and ad types, and to clarify any terminology or language that may be used going forward. As mentioned in the preface and introduction, this is not a detailed how-to guide on the mechanics of ad creation, campaign management, or using Facebook's interfaces and tools, so we will keep those details to a minimum. Still, it is good for every business owner to understand the basic core concepts, so that even if you work with a staff member, consultant or agency to run your ad campaigns, you have common ground for discussion.

Facebook Terminology

To ensure we are on common ground, or if you are rusty on some of Facebook's language, let's clarify some terminology.

Profile: Every person who signs up on Facebook creates a personal profile. Your profile includes personal information you choose to provide (age, birthday, where you live, relationship status, etc.) plus your Timeline or Wall (where your status updates and posts show up). Generally, only friends can see your profile and timeline, but that depends on your privacy and security settings. A profile must be a real person and is for non-commercial use only. To use Facebook in any capacity (including advertising), you must have a personal profile established.

Page: Pages looks similar to personal profiles, but are designed for businesses, brands, and organizations. Brands can include celebrities, athletes and public figures, thus these are often referred to as "fan pages". A person can only have one personal profile but can create and manage multiple pages. Pages can be "liked" by fans or followers, and when a post is made by a Page, it will show up in its followers' News Feeds. As a business, you will want to establish a Facebook Page.

News Feed: Your News Feed is where all the posts and status updates appear from your friends and the pages that you follow. When you log in to Facebook, you're News Feed is essentially your home page.

Ad creative: Creative (as a noun) refers to all the visual aspects of an ad: the image, video, border, text or sales copy, etc.

For a complete glossary of terms provided by Facebook, you can visit

www.facebook.com/help/219443701509174/

or refer to our free resources guide available in our book bonuses, where we provide a list of handy reference links.

Advertising Objectives

The very first step when creating a new ad campaign is choosing your advertising objective. Your objective is what you want people to do when they see your ad, which helps

Facebook optimize your ad for best results. Here are the choices you will see:

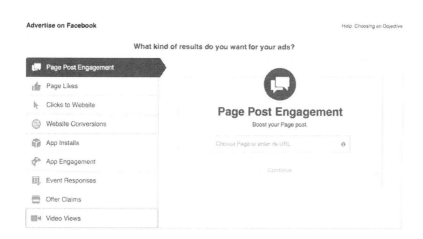

A brief explanation follows:

Page Post Engagement - Promote your Page Posts (so your content is seen more widely by your existing followers)

Page Likes - Get likes for your Page to grow your followers and audience

Clicks to Website - Get people to visit your website

Website Conversions - Promote specific conversions for your website

App Installs - Get people to install your desktop or mobile app

App Engagement - Get people to use your desktop app

Event Responses - Get people to attend your event

Offer Claims - Create offers for people to redeem in your store

Video Views - Create ads with Video

Again, the intent is not to go in-depth on each of these, but many are expanded upon when referenced in examples and other sections of this book.

Ad Placement

An ad can appear in three places on Facebook: in the Desktop News Feed, Mobile News Feed, or the Right Column of the Desktop page. At the time of ad creation, you specify which location you want it to appear (including all three). Facebook will optimize the look of the ad so that it appears at its best in each location. The key benefit of the two News Feed style ads is that they will appear right along with other posts in your audience's News Feed, and allow them to engage with the ad (like, share, comment) which increases its effectiveness. A quick visual of the three ad locations are below, courtesy of Facebook's Ads Product Guide:[11]

Facebook Ad Placements

Desktop News Feed and Right Column

Mobile News Feed

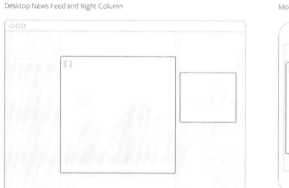

Summary

What we've covered in this chapter is a brief overview of some key terms and topics that will be referenced in other parts of this book. Obviously, we've just scratched the surface from an overall "ads overview" perspective, and complete coverage of every aspect could be a separate book in itself. However, anytime you are ready to dive into more details, you can go to the main Facebook Help page at www.facebook.com/help/ and choose "Facebook Ads" in the left menu.

Additionally, you will find a number of helpful resources available for free in the back of this book.

For easy access to the links above and additional resources available for free, be sure to visit:

www.perfectaudiencebook.com/bonus

Or

Text your name and email address to 415-691-BOOK (2665)

Or

Text the word PERFECT to x58885

Part Two

Chapter 5

Target Audience Selection

In the first section of this book we established why Facebook is such a promising advertising platform and why it should be an essential part of your paid media and traffic acquisition strategy. In part two of this book, we will look in depth at what truly sets Facebook apart: the wealth of data it has about its users, and the ability to target them utilizing that data. From user profile information they voluntarily provide, to their interests, actions, and behaviors expressed through likes, shares, comments, connections, groups joined, events attended, apps downloaded and other activities (even outside of Facebook, based on partner data that Facebook utilizes), these collectively supply a rich tapestry of data that you can harness when targeting your ideal audience.

Whereas in the past you may have given little thought about the interests and likes of your customers (what magazines they read, celebrities they follow, music they listen to, sports they play, hobbies they have, organizations or clubs they belong to, etc.), now all of these insights can be very beneficial and relevant when identifying and reaching out to your target market.

In this section we devote several chapters to walking through the audience selection criteria provided in Facebook. Before we dive in, let's say a few words about audience size.

Audience Size

As you go through the process of selecting your audience, Facebook displays a nice graphical representation of your audience size and the criteria used to derive that size. As you add or remove filters, the meter indicates how your audience definition either narrows or expands, and the potential reach adjusts at the bottom. Keep in mind that the numbers presented is an estimate only and not an exact figure.

Audience Definition

 Your audience is defined.

Specific   Broad

Audience Details:
- Location - Living In:
    - California, United States
- Age:
    - 35 - 50
- Gender:
    - female
- Relationship Status:
    - Married
- Moms:
    - Stay-at-home moms
- Placements:
    - on News Feed and right column on desktop computers, Mobile Feed and Third-party Apps

Potential Reach: 40,000 people

As we present various examples throughout the remainder of this book, we will often mention the potential audience reach, so now you know where this number is derived. Furthermore, for certain categories within demographics, interests, and behaviors, Facebook will indicate the number of people interested in that topic or who fit that particular category overall (not taking into account your other filters). Just hover your mouse over the category value in the list and the data will display. For example, as illustrated below, there are over 3.3 million people in the US who fall into the "stay-at-home moms" category.

A common question asked is "How large should my audience be?" There is no single correct answer to this, as it largely depends on your campaign objectives and scope (discussed in section 1), whether you are targeting a local market or a larger geographic area (or no area at all, thus defaulting to the country level), and other factors. As for general guidelines, opinions will vary among seasoned experts. Some recommend between 50,000 to 100,000 to start; other suggest in the 500,000 range. Facebook recommends at least 10,000 "for adequate delivery and performance" of your ad, but again, that number may be too high or not relevant in the context of a small local business or a narrowly targeted niche. On the opposite end, a national brand running large campaigns will likely want to reach broad audiences in the millions. Of course, the amount of budget you have set aside for ad spend is also a factor. We'll continue to touch upon audience sizing as we cover the different selection options and review specific examples.

In the next chapter, we'll start with the two fundamental categories for defining your audience: location and demographics.

Before We Proceed...

As mentioned in the preface, it is worth noting again that all the information presented here is accurate and up-to-date at the time of publication. As Facebook endeavors to continuously improve and update its advertising options, the categories, category values, and other selection criteria outlined in the next few chapters may change over time. For this reason, you may find slight variations in the options and values listed in this book than what you will find in Facebook's ad manager interface when you actually set up your ad campaigns.

For a handy printout guide that summarizes many of the category options and valued described in the next few chapters, be sure to visit:

www.perfectaudiencebook.com/bonus

Or

Text your name and email address to 415-691-BOOK (2665)

Or

Text the word PERFECT to x58885

Chapter 6

Locations and Demographics

Location targeting is the starting point for any audience selection, and is the first criteria you enter when setting up an ad. You can enter one or more of the following:

Country

State/Province

City

Zip Code

City targeting is not available in all countries, and zip codes only apply in the United States. At least one geographic selection is required when choosing an audience, and technically all other criteria can be left blank to place an ad. One nice feature is that you can select a mile radius for a given city to include nearby areas, such as "Chicago +10 miles" (10, 25, and 50 miles are the options). This could be particularly helpful if your business was in a small town and you wanted to ensure your ad reached everyone in the adjacent towns and larger surrounding area.

You can also use *exclusion targeting* to leave out specific locations within its larger geographic context. For example, you can target all of California but exclude Los Angeles and San Diego. Or start with the city of Los Angeles but exclude a select number of zip codes within to target a narrower area.

Local Marketing Benefits

Targeting specific cities or zip codes is a fantastic opportunity for local business marketing, allowing you to first set up a "geo boundary" and then apply further criteria to target your audience within that physical region.

For a small business that primarily focuses on its local community and neighborhood like a hardware store, florist, dry cleaner or salon; or perhaps a real estate agent, chiropractor, or dentist serving a city or county, this provides a number of benefits, including only putting your ad in front of the people that matter to you. You will get more value from your ad spend with a more accurate reach.

Contrast this with running an ad in a metropolitan-wide newspaper or on a local radio station. With a daily readership of over 1.4 million people, how likely is it that your "Summer Clearance Sale" ad buried on page 9 of section B in the Los Angeles Times will be seen by the 30-block radius of readers around your store who matter most? Furthermore, how much money did you spend putting that ad in front of 1.4 million pairs of eyes who aren't even your target customers? This is known as "waste circulation" in the advertising world. Alternately, how likely is it that your target customers will be listening to the very station and during the exact time slot when your 30 second radio spot airs?

As stated in the opening chapter, this isn't a blanket indictment against all forms of traditional advertising. They certainly have their place within a larger marketing strategy, as does other offline direct-response marketing options that are applicable for local businesses like direct mail. But with just the location targeting options alone, the advantages Facebook provides in reaching your ideal audience give you a strong "leg up" over other advertising mediums, and can be done with a very modest budget. The good news is, this is just the very beginning! Let's continue.

Demographics

These filters target people based on age, gender, relationship status, profession, education, life events, and other affiliations. Let's explore the top thirteen categories currently available and the subcategories within each.

TIP! A lot of information will be presented in these upcoming sections, but I encourage you to read through all the category and subcategory choices at least once. Even if initially you don't think a particular category or criteria will apply to your particular situation, you may be amazed at all the different options that are available to you, and it will likely stimulate your thinking and creativity about what's possible.

Plus, what's not applicable initially for one ad campaign may totally apply at another time for a different campaign or segment of your audience. Even if you hand off all your advertising management to an agency, consultant or staff member, it's always good to have a full awareness and understanding of all of the options available to you.

Age

Enter an age range between 13 - 64. The upper age can be left blank if desired.

Gender

Choices: Male, Female, or All

Language

Enter one or more languages that your audience speaks, or leave blank.

Relationship

Interested In

Choices: All, Men, Women, Men and Women, Unspecified

You can target people interested in a specific gender for networking, friendships, dating, or relationships.

Relationship Status

Choices: Single, In a relationship, Married, Engaged, Unspecified, Civil Union, Domestic Partnership, Open Relationship, Complicated, Separated, Divorced, Widowed

Education

Education Level

Choices: Associate degree, College grad, Doctorate degree, High school grad, In college, In grad school, In high school, Master's degree, Professional degree, Some college, Some grad school, Some high school, Unspecified

Fields of Study

Enter one or more majors or fields of study. Facebook will provide suggestions as you begin to type.

Schools

Enter the names of one or more schools at any level. Facebook will provide suggestions as you begin to type.

Undergrad Years

Enter a year or range of years when people graduated from college

Work

Employers

Enter the name of an employer or employers. Facebook will provide suggestions as you begin to type.

Job Titles

Enter one or more job titles. Facebook will provide suggestions as you begin to type.

Industries

Choices: Administrative; Architecture and Engineering; Arts, entertainment, sports and media; Business and financial operations; Cleaning and maintenance; Community and social services; Computer and mathematics; Construction and extraction; Education and library; Farming, fishing, and forestry; Food preparation and services; Healthcare and medical; IT and technical; Installation and repair; Legal; Management; Military; Personal care; Production; Protective Service; Retail; Sales; Science; Temporary and seasonal; Transportation and moving

Office Type (partner data, US only)

Choices: Corporation, Home office, Small office

Financial

Income (partner data, US only)

Target people based on their likely household income level.

Choices: $30-40K, $40-50K, $50-75K, $75-100K, $100-125K, over $125K

Net Worth (partner data, US only)

Target people based on their likely net worth.

Choices: $1 – $100,000; $100,000 – $1,000,000; $1,000,000 – $2,000,000; over $2,000,000

Home

Home Type (partner data, US only)

Choices: Multi-family home, single-family home

Home Ownership (partner data, US only)

Choices: Homeowners, Renters

Home Value (partner data, US only)

Choices: less than $50K; $50,000 - $99,999; $100,000 - $149,999 and continues in $50K range increments up to $500K; $500K - $599K; $600K - $699K and continues in $100K increments up to $1M; $1M - $1.49M; $1.5M - $1.99M; over $1.9M

Household Composition (partner data, US only)

Choices: Children in home, empty nesters, grandparents, new teen drivers, no children in home, veterans in home, working women, young adults in home

Ethnic Affinity

Choices: Hispanic US-All, Hispanic US-Bilingual, Hispanic US – English Dominant, Hispanic US – Spanish Dominant

Generation (US only)

Choices: Baby boomers, Generation X, Millennials

Parents

All Parents

Choices: Expectant parents, Parents (All), Parents (child: 0-3 yrs), Parents (child: 4-12 yrs), Parents (child: 13-15 yrs), Parents (child: 16-19 yrs)

Moms (partner data, US only)

Choices: Big-city moms, Corporate moms, Fit moms, Green moms, Soccer moms, Stay-at-home moms, Trendy moms

Politics

Choices: Donate to conservative political causes, Donate to liberal political causes, Registered voters (Democrat), Registered voters (Independent), Registered voters (Republican), US Politics (Active), US Politics (Conservative), US Politics (Liberal), US Politics (Moderate), US Politics (Very Conservative), US Politics (Very Liberal)

Life Events

Choices: Away from family, Away from hometown, Long distance relationship, New job, New relationship, Newly engaged (1 year), Newly engaged (3 months), Newly engaged (6 months), Newlywed (1 year), Newlywed (3 months), Newlywed (6 months), Recently moved, Upcoming birthday

This completes the current list of demographic categories and subcategories. As you may have noticed, some categories are based on external third-party partner data. We'll discuss this in more detail in the Behaviors chapter. Also, keep in mind that when setting up your audience definition for a particular campaign, you can select and combine as many locations, demographics, interests and behavior categories as appropriate, allowing you to get as narrow or broad as needed.

Next, we'll discuss one of the more powerful audience selection criteria Facebook offers - Interests!

Chapter 7

Interests

Interest filters are based on people's expressed interests, hobbies, and pages they like on Facebook, as well as information based on ads they've clicked on, apps they use, content posted on their timelines, and keywords associated with pages they've liked.

There are two ways to utilize Interests. First, Facebook provides a list of broad top level categories that you can browse, each of which have further subcategories 2 or 3 levels deep. There are hundreds of subcategories provided, all listed in their entirety here. The second way you can use Interests is to type in your own term, keyword, or page name to search for specific items. We'll cover each of these in this chapter.

The top-level categories of Interests are:

- Business & Industry
- Entertainment
- Family & Relationships
- Fitness & Wellness
- Food & Drink
- Hobbies & Activities
- Shopping & Fashion
- Sports & Outdoors
- Technology

Now let's look at the subcategories within these. If a subcategory has its own next level of options, those will be in parentheses.

Business & Industry

Advertising, Agriculture, Architecture, Aviation, Banking (Investment banking, Online banking, Retail banking), **Business, Construction, Design** (Fashion, design, Graphic design, Interior design), **Economics, Engineering, Entrepreneurship, Healthcare, Higher education, Management, Marketing, Nursing, Online** (Digital marketing, Display marketing, Email marketing, Online advertising, Search engine optimization, Social media, Social media marketing, Web design, Web development, Web hosting) **Personal finance** (Credit cards, Insurance, Investment, Mortgage loans), **Real estate, Retail, Sales, Science, Small business**

Entertainment

Games (Action game, Board games, Browser games, Card games, Casino games, First-person shooter games, Gambling, Massively multiplayer, Massively multiplayer role-playing, Online games, Online poker, Puzzle video games, Racing games, Role-playing games, Shooter games, Simulation games, Sports games, Strategy games, Video games, Word games, etc), **Live Events** (Ballet, Bars, Concerts, Dance halls, Music festivals, Nightclubs, Parties, Plays, Theater), **Movies** (Action, Animated, Bollywood, Comedy, Documentary, drama, fantasy,

Horror, musical, science-fiction, thrillers), **Music** (Blues, Classical, Country, Dance, Electronic, Gospel, Heavy Metal, Hip hop, Jazz, Music videos, Pop, Rhythm and blues, Rock, Soul), **Reading** (Books, Comics, E-Books, Fiction, Literature, Magazines, Manga, Mystery, Newspapers, Nonfiction, Romance), **TV** (Comedies, game shows, reality shows, talk shows_)

Family and Relationships

Dating, family, fatherhood, friendship, marriage, motherhood, parenting, weddings

Fitness and Wellness

Bodybuilding, dieting, Gyms, meditation, nutrition, Physical exercise, physical fitness, running, weight loss, weight training, yoga, Zumba

Food and Drink

Alcoholic beverages (Beer, distilled beverage, wine), **beverages** (Coffee, energy drinks, juice, soft drinks, Tea), **cooking** (Baking, recipes), **cuisine** (Chinese, French, German, Greek, Indian, Italian, Japanese, Korean, Latin America, Mexican, Middle Eastern, Spanish, Thai, Vietnamese), **food** (Barbecue, chocolate, desserts, fast food, organic food, pizza, seafood, veganism, vegetarianism), **restaurants** (Cafés, coffeehouses, diners, fast casual, fast food)

Hobbies and Activities

Arts and music (acting, crafts, dance, drawing, drums, fine art, guitar, painting, performing arts, photography, sculpture, singing, writing), **current events, home and Garden** (Do it yourself (DIY), furniture, gardening, home appliances, home-improvement), **Pets** (Birds, cats, dogs, Fish, horses, pet food, rabbits, reptiles), **politics and social issues** (Charity and causes, community issues, environmentalism, law, military, politics, religion, sustainability, veterans, volunteering), **travel** (Adventure travel, air travel, beaches, car rentals, cruises, ecotourism, hotels, lakes, mountains, nature, sightseeing, theme parks, vacations), **vehicles** (Automobiles, boats, electric vehicle, hybrids, minivans, motorcycles, RVs, SUVs, scooters, trucks)

Shopping and Fashion

Beauty (Beauty salons, cosmetics, fragrances, hair products, spas, tattoos), **clothing** (Children's, men's, shoes, women's), **fashion accessories** (Dresses, handbags, jewelry, sunglasses), **shopping** (Boutiques, coupons, discount stores, luxury goods, online shopping, shopping malls), **toys**

Sports and Outdoors

Outdoor recreation (Boating, camping, fishing, hiking, horseback riding, hunting, mountain biking, surfing) , **sports** (American football, Association football (Soccer), auto racing, baseball, basketball, college football, golf, marathons, skiing, snowboarding, swimming, tennis, triathlons, volleyball)

Technology

Computers (memory, monitors, processors, servers, desktop computers, free software, hard drives, network storage, software, tablet computers), **consumer electronics** (audio equipment, camcorders, cameras, e-book readers, GPS devices, gaming consoles, mobile phones, portable media players, projectors, smartphones, televisions)

In summary, the categories provided by Facebook are both numerous and broad. Depending upon the goals of your ad campaign, the breadth and all-inclusive scope of some of these categories may be advantageous if you are trying to greatly expand your audience reach. More likely however, you will be better served by targeting more specific interests and likes of your audience. This can be done with precise interests.

Precise Interests

In the past, Facebook had separate fields for broad interests and precise interests, but now they are merged. Instead of selecting from the list of categories and subcategories described previously, you can simply type in any keyword, term, phrase, interest, or existing page name and find millions of additional attributes and suggestions. You can enter as many keywords and categories in the Interests field, as you want. Keep in mind that doing so will expand your audience reach because Facebook will target anyone who likes A *or* B, not just people who like both A and B. Currently, targeting people who only fall into both (or all) categories is not possible.

Gym Owner Example

Let's illustrate with a couple examples to see what's possible with precise interests. Let's say you are the owner of a local gym and this is a "no frills" establishment catering to hardcore bodybuilders. In other words, you have no yoga classes or children's play area here! Given this is a local business, you would start by choosing an appropriate location, either by city or zip code.

Your target market is primarily male, although you would certainly welcome female bodybuilders as members. From an optimization perspective, you only want to place your ads in front of those to whom it would appeal the most. So if you want to reach both sexes, you should run two separate ads -- one targeting males and the other females, which would allow you to tailor the ad creative (images & copy) to speak specifically to those demographics. The images and language used to attract and appeal to a female audience would likely be much different than a male (though not always, of course.)

Continuing on, you would next go to Interests, and by looking under Fitness and Wellness you might be tempted to pick Bodybuilding (54,166,700 people) or Weight training (40,048,300 people). The numbers provided by Facebook when you highlight each entry are in their words "people who have expressed an interest in or like pages related to" those interests. (Please note those numbers are prior to any additional filter criteria you may have applied yourself, and are global in nature, unless specified otherwise.)

To get some real numbers in this example, let's set our audience definition to "San Diego + 10 miles" targeting Men ages 18 and over. With both Bodybuilding and Weight training chosen as Interests, our potential reach is 64,000 people. Not bad!

However, let's say you don't want to go after people with just a general interest in these areas. You really want to hone in on those serious bodybuilders who are committed to working out religiously and need your awesome gym facilities to achieve their goals! You want the hardcore passionate guys who eat, sleep and breathe this stuff. Keep in mind -- we don't know exactly how these 64,000 were ultimately tagged (or the 40 and 54 million globally for that matter). Yes, they've "expressed an interest in or liked pages related to" these two subjects, but that could be of a passive nature. Perhaps they clicked on an ad, liked a friend's post or page, or a random link related to bodybuilding or weight training and that classified them with these interests. That's not to say they wouldn't be good potential customers, but your objective is to target only those who are highly predisposed to signing up for a gym membership in a facility like yours, and as a small business owner, you have no marketing budget to waste on those who might only be mildly interested.

What do you do? Take advantage of precise interests by considering what profile makes up your ideal customer in this case. What magazines do these guys read? How about Muscle & Fitness or Flex! Let's start there. Replacing the two categories above with these precise interests cuts the reach in half to 34,000. Using just Flex Bodybuilding Magazine by itself drops it further to 24,000.

If you wanted to broaden your reach based on magazines, you could add a third like Men's Health (48,000), which is tailored to perhaps a less hardcore but still appropriate segment of men. To reiterate the idea here, while many men might have an interest in weight training, it's more probable that those who follow and "like" these specific magazine pages (and who presumably subscribe) are more serious and hardcore about bodybuilding.

What else would serious bodybuilders be passionate about with their interests? Perhaps they follow well-known bodybuilders' fan pages like Lou Ferrigno (17,400) or Arnold Schwarzenegger (16,200). Of course, since both of these men are actors as well and Arnie's a former politician to boot, they'll have much broader fan bases and thus may not be the most appropriate choices. (You can tell I'm stretching my knowledge here on this subject, so insert your favorite body builder or Mr. Olympia name appropriately.)

Other options? How about fans of the bodybuilding documentary Pumping Iron (14,000)? Or fans of specific brands of supplements, clothing lines, weightlifting equipment, gear and accessories, books and videos? Or, target an online e-commerce website selling all of the above like bodybuilding.com (34,000)? How about people who've liked the International Federation of BodyBuilding & Fitness (IFBB) page? Those likely are some serious weight lifters!

With each of the interests examples above, the overall reach ranged from a low of 3.9 million people (Pumping Iron) to over 16.3 million people (Muscle & Fitness), but when additionally filtered through the "San Diego Males over 18" criteria, we had a nice range of approximately 15,000 to 60,000 to work with.

I may have exhausted this particular example but I wanted to illustrate the vast array of options and different directions you can explore when using interests to target your audience, and to re-emphasize again how valuable it is to understand the demographics, psychographics, and profiles of your ideal customers as much as possible. In this case however, I purposely picked a subject that I knew very little, if anything, about. But with a little bit of research and digging deeper into this market, I started surfacing ideas & criteria that would likely work very well.

Want to learn more about how to do this effectively yourself? I have a whole chapter dedicated to research methods and tools for discovering insights about your perfect audience later in this book.

Suggested Interests

There's one more thing worth highlighting about how Interests work. Since you can enter any free form text or phrase into the Interests field, Facebook will provide suggestions as you type, matching your phrase with what it has on record and provide related suggestions that you may have never considered! This is quite powerful because it's based on real data of all the pages and activity ever performed on Facebook. Remember, anyone can create as many pages as they want on Facebook (in addition to their personal profile), so it's not uncommon to find multiple pages and many variations around a popular interest, person, or topic.

For example, I only referred to the official Muscle & Fitness entry above that had a global reach of over 16.3 million people. What I didn't mention were variations I found, including "muscle fitness magazine" with a 1.1 million reach. Is that entry related to the brand-verified page of the magazine itself? Possibly not. But, it's another 1.1 million people that is a likely subset of the larger one, but perhaps contains some percentage of people who aren't. When we include that smaller interest by itself in the context of the "San Diego Males over 18" filter, our potential reach drops from the thirty thousand range to only 1,800 people. Are these the super highly targeted audience that the gym owner is after? Perhaps! As recommended for any advertising campaign, you will want to test multiple ads and to different segments. Run one ad to this smaller group and another ad to the larger group and compare results. Or, combine the two to ensure you're reaching the greatest number of people if that is your goal.

Cooking Example

To illustrate the list of suggestions Facebook provides with one final example, let's say you are a cookbook author ready to promote your latest release on Italian cooking. For sake of simplicity, you target the US market only with no other age or demographics identified initially, since you are just in research mode at this point. Starting with the Interests categories Facebook provides, you pick Food & Drink -> Cuisine -> Italian, which has a reach of 17.2 million in the US. You then replace this category and type in the word "pasta", and your reach drops significantly to 4.2 million. If that happens to be your book's focus, this is a good thing!

Now, let's say your ad will offer a free copy of the best old-world spaghetti recipe ever created, so you type in "spaghetti" and find your audience narrows further to 960,000. Think about that for a moment. Almost one million people (and over 4.2 million globally) have explicitly or implicitly shown powerful interest in ...spaghetti!

But here's where it gets even more fun and interesting. As you type in the keyword spaghetti, Facebook provides a list of related suggestions based on the data it has. As you can see in the picture below, this includes SpaghettiOs (a brand), spaghetti with meatballs or spaghetti Bolognese (specific dishes), Spaghetti Warehouse (a restaurant) and even spaghetti strap (fashion) and spaghetti westerns (movies)!

Who would have guessed that over 200,000 people have an interest in spaghetti straps! Not relevant at all for a cookbook promotion, but perhaps good insight for a fashion designer or clothing retailer? As you can see, the options you have are almost endless, and using Interests is a fantastic way to really hone in on the likes, activities, and topics that matter most to your audience.

If Interests weren't enough to get you excited, how about tapping into what people like to do *off* of Facebook, like reaching those who are in the market for a new car, or who like to shop for premium pet food, or buy natural and organic products, or who own a particular model smartphone, or have expressed interest in traveling to Brazil? These amazing insights are available through Behaviors, which we'll cover in the next chapter.

Chapter 8

Behaviors and Connections

Behaviors are based on activities that people do on or *off* Facebook that reflect things like purchase behavior or intent, device usage, travel preferences and more. For example, you can target people who are in the market for a new car, and even narrow it down to specific makes and models! Or you can reach existing owners of particular makes and models and even target by how long ago they purchased and whether it was new or used. You can target people who like to donate to particular political, environmental, religious, or other charitable causes. You can tap deeply into the digital and mobile worlds, segmenting your audiences by which operating systems they use, browsers used, whether they actively spend money online, what mobile devices they use (down to specific models), or broadly target all IOS users, Android users, smartphone users, or tablet users. If you do anything in the hardware, software, mobile apps, gaming, or phone accessories space, this data could be invaluable for you.

Purchase behavior is also extremely rich. You can select audiences based on broad buyer profiles (fashionistas, foodies, luxury brands, etc.); a variety of clothing and apparel categories for men, women, and children; food and drink categories, health and beauty, home and garden, and household product categories; pet products; sports products; and even where people like to shop (high-end retail, home improvement stores, etc.) Finally, there are residential profiles and travel categories that allow you to target vacationers, business travelers, particular destinations, and more.

How do they gather all of this data, particularly from websites outside of Facebook? Facebook currently works with three trusted third-party partners Acixom, Datalogix, and Epsilon in a privacy-safe way to construct these behavior categories via transactional data, survey information, and other online and offline activity. User profiles on Facebook are anonymously matched with this data in a way that advertisers can never receive or access personal information or target specific people. Some other categories within Demographics and Interests discussed in previous chapters are also sourced from these partners whenever data is not self-reported by the user, such as income levels and home value. DLX Auto, a partnership between Datalogix and Polk, provides all automotive data. Please note that most of this data is available for the US only.

The top-level Behavior categories include:

- Automotive
- Charitable donations
- Digital activities
- Financial
- Mobile Device User
- Purchase behavior
- Residential profiles
- Travel

As with the Interests chapter, we will list as many subcategories and sub-subcategory details as possible, except where noted. Again, we recommend you do at least a one-pass read through all the information so that you have a solid understanding of the kind of data available to you when targeting your audience.

Automotive

Motorcycle, New vehicle buyers (Near market), new vehicle shoppers (in market), owners, purchase type, Used vehicle buyers (in market)

Since the automotive category is quite extensive, it will be more conducive to explain how its subcategories are set up, rather than list every single selection. In the **New vehicle buyers** category, "Near market" means a household is considering a purchase within the next year (365 days). The subcategories within are based on style, which include Crossover, Economy/compact, full-size SUV, full-size sedan, Hybrid/alternative fuel, luxury SUV, luxury sedan, midsize car, minivan, pickup truck, small/midsize SUV, and sports car/convertible.

The "**new vehicle shoppers (in market)**" category are those households who are likely to buy within the next 180 days. Its subcategories are broken out by Make (with over 33 car brands listed), Model (over 50 specific models like Ford F150 or Honda Accord), and the same Style options listed above.

Under the **owners** category, you will find breakdowns by make, aftermarket purchase behavior (auto parts, service, etc), purchased time frame (0-6 months ago, 7-12 months ago, etc), vehicle age, vehicle price ranges, and style.

Purchase type covers whether they plan to lease, buy new, buy used, buy new or used, and then each of those are further classified by in market (180 days) or near market (365 days).

Used vehicle buyers have the same Make and Style sub-categories as mentioned already, and finally the **motorcycle** category offers subcategories of owners by Make and Purchase window.

Charitable donations

All charitable donations, animal welfare, arts and cultural, children's interests, environmental and wildlife, health, political, religious, veterans, world relief

Digital activities

Console gamers, Facebook page admins, Internet browser used (chrome, Firefox, Internet Explorer, Opera, Safari), **online spenders, online spenders (active), online spenders (engaged), operating system used** (Mac OS X, Windows 7, Windows 8, Windows Vista, Windows XP), **small business owners, technology early adopters, technology late adopters, unity plug-in**

Financial

Insurance - auto insurance (renews in January, renews in February, etc. for all 12 months), **health insurance** (likely no dependents, likely to have dental insurance), **home insurance**

(expires in January, expires in February, etc. for all 12 months), **life insurance**

Investments (highly likely investors, likely full-service investors, likely investors, likely self-directed investors),

Spending methods (active credit card user, any card type, bank cards, gas, department and retail store cards, high-end department store cards, premium credit cards, primary cash, primary credit cards, travel and entertainment cards)

Mobile Device User

All mobile devices by brand - **Apple** (all iPad, iPod, and iPhone models listed), **BlackBerry** (multiple models listed), **Google** (Nexus 5), **HTC, Huawei, LG** (multiple models listed), **Motorola, Nokia** (multiple models listed), **other Android devices, Samsung** (multiple models listed), **Sony**

All mobile devices by operating system (all Android devices, all IOS devices, Windows phones),

All mobile devices, feature phones, network connection (2G, 3G, 4G)

New smart phone and tablet owners, smart phone owners, smart phones and tablets, tablet owners

Purchase Behavior

Business purchases (Business marketing, maintenance, repair and operations, office and corporate gifts, training and publications)

Buyer profiles (DIYers, fashionistas, foodies, gadget enthusiast, gamers, green living, healthy and fit, luxury brands and services, outdoor enthusiasts, shoppers, skiing golfing and voting, sponsorships, sportsman, trendy home makers)

Clothing - **children's** (children's apparel, infant and toddler apparel), **men's** (accessories, big and tall, business apparel, jeans), **seasonal** (fall seasonal shoppers, Spring, Summer, Winter), **women's** (accessories, business apparel, fine jewelry, high ticket apparel and accessories, jewelry, low ticket apparel and accessories, luxury brand apparel, mid ticket apparel and accessories, plus sizes, women's shoes, Young women's apparel)

Food and drink - **alcoholic beverages** (beer, spirits, wine), **bakery, beverages** (bottled water, carbonated drinks, coffee, coffee(take-up), **diet drinks, energy drinks, hot tea, iced tea and lemonade, juice, non-dairy milk, sports drinks, cereal** (all cereal, children's cereals, fiber cereals, hot cereals), **children's food** (baby food and products, children's food, children's food and products), **condiments and dressings** (condiments, salad dressing), **cooking supplies** (baking, spices), **dairy and eggs** (cheese, eggs, milk, yogurt), **frozen food** (frozen entrées, frozen meat and seafood, frozen vegetables, ice cream and novelties), **grocery shopper type** (premium brand groceries, top spenders), **health food** (diet foods, fresh produce, low-fat foods, natural and organic), **meat and seafood, soup, sweets and snacks** (breakfast bars, chocolate candy, cookies, crackers, granola bars, non-chocolate candy, peanut butter and jelly, salty snacks)

Health and beauty (allergy relief, beauty products and accessories, cosmetics, cough and cold relief, fragrance, hair care, over-the-counter medication, pain relief, sun care, vitamins and supplements), **home and Garden** (Entertaining, home renovation, organization, tools)

Household products (Cleaning supplies, food storage, Green cleaners and supplies, laundry supplies)

Kids products (Baby care, baby toy, children's products)

Pet products (Cat food and products, cat owners, cat products, dog food and products, dog owners, dog products,, Pet care products, Pet products)

Purchase habits (above average spending, off-line buyers, online buyers)

Purchase types (appliances, arts and crafts, Beauty accessories, books, Collectibles, cosmetics, electronics, gender neutral apparel, Gift products, gifts and party supplies, high-end home decor, home office, Low-end home decor, Men's apparel, music and videos, senior products, shoes, small and home office products, Software, specialty foods and gifts, sports and outdoors, tools and electronics, travel supplies, upscale travel and services, women's apparel)

Sports and outdoors (cycling, fishing, Fitness, golf and tennis, hiking and camping, hunting, running, winter sports)

Store types (furniture stores, high-end retail, home-improvement stores, low-end department stores, Membership warehouse)

Subscription services (auto insurance online, higher education, mortgage online, prepaid debit cards, satellite TV)

Residential Profiles

Likely to move, recent homebuyer, recent mortgage borrower, recently moved

Travel

All frequent travelers, business travelers, business travelers international, business travelers US, Casino vacations, commuters, cruises, currently traveling, family vacations, frequent fliers, leisure travelers, personal travelers International, Personal travelers US

Planning to travel (intender– any destination, intender – Australia, intender – beach, intender – Brazil, etc. for key countries and cities)

Return from trip 1 week ago, return from trip 2 weeks ago, timeshares, use travel app - 1 month, Used travel app - 2 weeks

Behaviors Summary

As you can see, the categories and subcategories (and sub-subcategories!) under Behaviors are quite extensive. They obviously don't apply to everyone, but if your particular business focus or target audience falls into one of these areas, then imagine how powerful it would be to have access to data like this at your fingertips. Normally these large data providers cater to big ad agencies and other firms who spend serious money for purchase and behavioral data like this. Now you — the "small time" operator — are on equal footing with the big boys. Facebook truly levels the playing field, providing anyone with a desire to reach a particular audience with all the data and capabilities normally only available to those with large financial resources to acquire it.

Connections

Finally, Facebook gives you connection-related targeting options, whereby you can target people who are connected to your Facebook page, Facebook app, or any Facebook event that you've set up. This is great for reaching out exclusively to your existing fan base, event attendees, or app owners.

Secondly, you can extend that reach by targeting friends of people you have a connection with, or "friends of friends." This is often a good strategy because people often share the same interests as their friends, and those people are more inclined to connect with you (via your page, app, or event) if they know their friends are connected as well. If you've ever seen a Facebook ad promoting a particular page, and included above the ad are names of your friends who've also liked this page — you are seeing a direct result of this option being used. The familiar names add social proof and relevancy to the ad, increasing the chances that you will interact and take whatever action it is calling you to do.

Finally, you have an exclusion option to only target people who are *not* connected to you currently. This is great for expanding your audience, reaching out to new people, and not putting an existing ad or offer in front of people who may have already attended, downloaded your app, or liked your page.

In summary, I hope you see the power and almost endless combination of locations, demographics, interests, behaviors, and connections you can use to target and segment your ideal audience. Any discussion about reaching your perfect audience would not be complete without reviewing three other advanced targeting capabilities within Facebook. We'll cover these next.

Chapter 9

Custom Audiences

"Sometimes the most valuable audience is the one you already have a connection with." - Facebook

Custom audiences, Website custom audiences, and their derivative sister Lookalike audiences are arguably the three most powerful capabilities within the Facebook advertising platform. In a nutshell, custom audiences let you advertise to people you already know, targeting the portion of your existing, offline audiences who are also on Facebook. Your "existing offline audiences" can consist of your email list, leads or prospects list, customer database list, visitors to your website, or people who have downloaded your mobile app (IOS, Android, or apps utilizing the Facebook SDK).

Facebook lets you create a custom audience by using either email addresses, phone numbers, Facebook user IDs or mobile advertiser IDs, and you do so by uploading a simple text or CSV file containing a single column of data with no header. Without getting too technical, Facebook creates a secured encrypted hash of your data upon uploading, creating the equivalent of a digital fingerprint for each entry. It then compares this hashed fingerprint against the corresponding hashed fingerprints it stores for all its users on Facebook to find matching IDs. This way, Facebook never sees or stores your actual viewable data (emails or phone numbers) on its servers, alleviating any security or privacy concerns. Custom Audiences based on website visitors are set up in a different manner, and will be addressed later in this chapter.

Facebook has specific terms and conditions that you must review and accept before creating your first custom audience. A word of caution: always (always!) play by the rules and never do anything that will push the boundaries or directly violate their terms of service. One of the primary objectives they want to ensure is that these are *your* lists that people have voluntarily agreed to opt-in to, thus giving you permission to market to them. For example, you can't upload rented or purchased lists from list brokers, or "scraped" Facebook IDs of individual users, or of audiences that Facebook themselves doesn't allow you to target directly (for example, members of public or private Facebook groups). If you are caught violating these terms, you risk your account getting banned. Many people have learned this the hard way; don't let this be you! Be sure to check our resources section for a link to Facebook's Terms of Service (available free when you access the book bonus page).

Data Sources and Lists

We've explained what Custom Audiences are, but before we dive into how to best use them, let's first discuss the available data sources you have to create them. The true benefits of custom audiences first start with how well the existing lists you already have can be segmented into different groupings based on their source, relationship status with your business, purchase activity, etc.

For example, you might have an active blog or website and are already building your email or newsletter list online. Great! Or perhaps you have one or more landing pages to capture leads with different free giveaway offers (your "lead magnets") that encourage people to opt-in. Each lead capture page builds your general list of leads, and ideally they are also set up to segment these leads into separate categories based on the particular campaign or offer they responded to.

If you sell products or services online, then a subset of your leads and prospects will eventually convert into customers, clients or patients. Ideally, your customer database will also have the ability to track and report individuals by their purchase history and time frame. The email marketing solution or CRM (Customer Relationship Management) software you have in place will determine to what extent you are able to track and segment a person through your entire marketing funnel (from visitor to lead to prospect to customer to repeat customer).

If you have yet to explore the full capabilities of the systems you utilize (or have none in place at all), I highly recommend doing so, or invest in your business by hiring the necessary expertise to have these systems installed and set up for you properly. The more you know about your own lists of leads and customers, what relationship you have with them, and where they are in the lifecycle of your product and service offerings, the more you will be able to tailor your messaging, targeting, and customize future offers to them. And, the more you will be able to take full advantage of the targeting and custom audience capabilities within Facebook.

What if you have a retail brick-and-mortar store, or run a private practice as a dentist, chiropractor, accountant, or other service professional and are more focused "offline"? This equally applies as well! Whether you have a modern Point of Sale (POS) solution with built-in sales and marketing functions; or a simple database or spreadsheet where you collect customer info; or even a manual tracking solution behind the front counter ("Is this your first time here?" "How did you hear about us?" and "Would you like to sign up on our mailing list?" all still work!), knowing *who* your customers are, *how often* they buy from you and *where* they came from are valuable insights that can be leveraged when reaching out to them again through targeted ads.

If you are just starting out and have no existing list to speak of, that's OK too! There are three immediate areas you can focus on. First, you can start building up your fan base for your Facebook page (which you can use ads to promote, if desired).

Secondly, and more strategically, you can use Facebook ads to drive traffic to your lead capture pages or website to start building your email list. If you've been exposed to any online or Internet marketing teachings of the last few years, then you have probably heard the saying, "The money's in the list." It's true that one of your business's most valuable assets is your list, or will become so if you are just beginning to create it.

Third, you will want to immediately take advantage of Website Custom Audiences discussed later in this chapter, which allows you to target any visitor to your website (even if they never join your email list or like your Facebook page), and use that as the basis of your ad targeting.

Tip! While list building, lead capture pages, and website design are beyond the scope of this book, they are critical components (what I call "marketing pillars") for creating a comprehensive online marketing strategy for your business. Be sure to check out the free resources at the end of this book if you want to learn more about these subjects.

Custom Audiences Usage

Now that we've discussed the importance of your data sources, let's explore the many ways you can use custom audiences. First, you can target your email list or newsletter subscribers who aren't currently fans on Facebook and ask them to like and follow your page. Perhaps you already do this in your newsletter template or in your email signature at the bottom (e.g. "Please like us on Facebook…"). The simple reality is that not everyone is going to take this action, no matter how often they see it in your messages. For one, the action can be disruptive because it takes them out of their email program and into their browser, straight into one of the largest time vampire social sites in existence! (After all, we *are* talking about Facebook, right?) Or perhaps they are quickly checking their email on their mobile device where the likelihood of clicking on your Facebook link from an email message is rather slim.

Contrast this with the times when they are consciously on Facebook doing, well, Facebook-like things. They are there to be social, to engage, to like, to share, to comment. Now imagine your ad shows up in their News Feed that reminds them how amazing and great your page is and asks them to like it. Click. Bam. Done. That was easy!

They already know you (since they are an email subscriber), they must like you to some degree (since they haven't unsubscribed yet!) and so it's very likely they would follow and like you on Facebook without a second thought. But now, you've made it super easy for them to say yes because you've reached out to them in the very environment where they are "in the mood" to do these things, and liking, commenting, and sharing is what people do all day long on this platform.

By the way, you may want to make sure to exclude your existing fans when running an ad for this purpose (using the option in the Connections filter discussed previously). There's no reason to ask your existing fans to like your page when they've already done it. It both unnecessarily wastes your ad spend and risks annoying your followers.

Secondly, you can target your email or newsletter subscribers with ads that promote a product, an event, or makes an announcement about a new blog post or new content on your website. You may be asking yourself "Why do this when I can just email them directly?", and probably already have?

While the death of email has been greatly exaggerated, the simple reality is that a huge percentage of emails never get opened and read. This can be for a variety of reasons and may have *nothing* to do with them not liking your content or not wanting to hear from you. Perhaps your email is never delivered properly or gets caught unexpectedly in their spam filter. Or, it gets buried amongst the hundreds of other unread messages crying out for their attention, and in one fell swoop it is swept into the trash with everything else, temporarily achieving those satisfying feelings of "inbox zero" nirvana and accomplishment. (So don't take it personally if your email goes unread!)

But now, by targeting your existing email list on Facebook, it's a sure way to reach out again and get your message or announcement in front of them that they may not see otherwise. It's also an excellent way to re-engage with them and drive them back to your website for new content, a special offer, or a promotion. Furthermore, the more often they see you in their News Feed or in the side bar, you are creating top-of-mind awareness — keeping your business, your brand, and message fresh in their consciousness.

Third, you can create a number of separate custom audiences based on different customer segments. Here are some examples to consider.

Create an audience of

- Active customers who have purchased recently, and offer them a limited time "thank you" discount if they return soon for more purchases.
- Active customers who buy frequently, and offer them membership into a new loyalty program with exclusive discounts.
- Prospects who haven't purchased yet and offer a special "New customer" discount.
- Customers who haven't purchased anything in the last 12 months, and you run ads to entice them back with a

special "We miss you" promotion or "Welcome back" sale.

Remember to expand these examples and brainstorm ways on how they could be applied in your own business or practice. For example, if you are a Dentist and can identify a list of past patients who haven't visited in over a year or two, this would be a fantastic way to entice them back. Imagine a "We haven't seen you in awhile! Come visit us again for a 25% off teeth cleaning special..." ad that appears in your News Feed. Combined with the right imagery and copy, these can be highly effective conversions because it's personal, it's coming from a known or familiar entity, and it doesn't come across as "salesy".

Or perhaps you are a Chiropractor or other health professional and you want to target inactive patients whom you haven't seen in awhile. You can offer a specially-priced "Wellness Checkup", or perhaps a 20-minute free massage on their next visit, or even a "bring a friend / refer a friend" discount that not only gets them to return, but brings in new referrals and business as well!

As you can see, there are many creative ways to use Custom Audiences, and the more ways you have to classify, categorize, and segment your existing lists of leads, prospects, customers, clients, and patients, the greater number of options you will have in targeting them.

In addition, you can still apply all of the other targeting filters on top of your Custom Audiences if appropriate. Let's say your list is national or international in scope, and you are promoting an event you are having in a particular city. You can select your custom audience to start and then apply a location filter to only target those list members in that city or zip code. Or perhaps you are promoting an offer that is particularly geared towards females only. You can apply whatever demographics, interests, or behavior categories you want on top of your custom audiences to get even more precise with your targeting.

Finally, custom audiences are also an excellent way to *exclude* existing customers or subscribers from seeing your ad. This is perfect when trying to only target new customers or grow your email list with new subscribers, so that you are not wasting money putting your ad in front of people who are already on your list. When picking your custom audiences during your ad campaign setup, this is where you can also identify one or more audiences to exclude.

Have a website but don't have a list? No problem! You've love the solution discussed in the next chapter.

Chapter 10

Website Custom Audiences & Retargeting

Reaching out to your existing lists is great, but now imagine being able to target all the visitors to your website or landing pages who have never opted in to your list, joined your newsletter, or made a purchase. Imagine being able to reach out and connect with those very same "anonymous" visitors on Facebook!

Maybe you are just starting out with a brand new website and have no list or customers at all. Or perhaps you've been creating great content on your website or blog for many months, have diligently worked to improve your search engine rankings to generate organic traffic, and have even dabbled in Google Adwords to pay for traffic. You check your analytics and know you're getting a consistent amount of visitors on a daily, weekly, or monthly basis, but you don't know how to leverage or capitalize on this traffic beyond the small percentage of those who join your list, become customers, or contact you directly.

Now imagine you can not only target all of these visitors, but you can further classify and target them independently based on which content or pages they viewed, which product categories, product pages, or sections they visited, and even how far they progressed through a sales checkout process and either completed the transaction or abandoned it. Sound too good to be true? Welcome to Facebook's Website Custom Audiences and the power of retargeting!

Retargeting

So what exactly is retargeting, also known as remarketing? Have you ever had the experience of visiting a retail website or large brand like Zappos, Amazon, or Nordstrom; or booked travel arrangements online; or researched a new service or product you might buy; or even accidentally clicked on an ad for something like a credit card? Then sometime later (even within minutes) you visit another website like CNN, Yahoo, other media outlet, or Facebook, and you now start seeing ads for Nordstrom, or the hotel you just booked or stayed at recently, or that new phone or wireless service you were just researching, or even more credit card ads? Sometimes the ad will even show a picture of the exact clothing item you were viewing a few minutes ago, or remind you that you placed an item in your shopping cart days ago but never checked out! (Beware; your ads may get even more interesting when shopping for your spouse!)

If this has happened to you, ta da — you've been retargeted! The first time you notice this, it can feel a little unnerving or spooky as if you're being digitally stalked. The reality however, is that unless you purposely browse in privacy mode or take extra steps to configure your online usage to be as anonymous as possible, then you are leaving trails behind you of virtually every place you visit online. And merchants and advertisers, who use these global ad networks that tie into all of these websites, will take full advantage of that trail and serve up ads intended to appeal to you. (For the record, the advertisers don't know that it is specifically *you* — John or Jane Smith. But it is tied to your specific browser (Chrome, Firefox, Safari, IE, etc.) and the IP address from your Internet service provider you are using. Simply switch browsers or clear all your cookies and they'll have no record that you were just shopping for those pair of shoes (until you do it again!).

Website Custom Audiences in Facebook

While global retargeting is beyond the scope of this book, Facebook gives you this same capability of identifying visitors who have previously been to your own website, and then retarget them when they appear again on Facebook. As illustrated in the examples at the beginning of this section, this is a very powerful capability with enormous potential, allowing you to custom tailor an ad specifically based on the website content or pages that they've previously viewed.

Setting up a Website Custom Audience is done in the ads manager tool and the process is fairly straightforward. Facebook will give you a custom audience remarketing pixel (a small snippet of JavaScript code used for tracking) that you install on your website just once, and in a way that it will be included in all of the pages of your site that you want tracked. If your website is built on a standard platform like Wordpress or other popular CMS, you typically only have to place this code once into the "head" section of your website theme, and it automatically propagates to every existing and future page that you create. If this sounds too complicated or technical, don't worry — simply copy the code Facebook gives you and hand it off to your web developer. The process is not difficult.

Once installed, Facebook will start building your website custom audience list automatically from that point forward based on any traffic you receive, and will continue to grow dynamically as more visitors come to your site over time. Facebook requires a minimum of 20 people in an audience before it can be used with an ad campaign, so the sooner you set this up, the better and more robust it will be at the time you are ready to target them. Finally, you must configure how long a person will remain in your website custom audience, which you can set up to a maximum of 180 days. After this time, the person will be removed automatically until they revisit the website again.

Facebook only gives one custom audience pixel per ad account, but you can set up different rules to define as many different audiences as you want based on the content of your website. Once you pick "Custom Audience from your Website" option in the Ads Manager, you will get the next screen below which shows five options for rules definition:

1. Anyone who visits your website
2. People who visit specific web pages
3. People visiting specific web pages but not others
4. People who haven't visited in a certain amount of time
5. Custom Combination

Create Audience   ✕

Website traffic ❔ | People who visit specific web pages ▼ |

           Anyone who visits your website   owing rules.
    ✓ People who visit specific web pages
       People visiting specific web pages but not others
       People who haven't visited in a certain amount of time

In the last ❔   Custom Combination

Audience Name   Men's Clothing
           Add a description

⚙   Cancel **Create Audience**

Using a clothing retail website as an example, let's assume you want to target men's clothing shoppers, and your website page structure looks like

Mystore.com/shopping/clothing/men/

Mystore.com/shopping/clothing/women/

Mystore.com/shopping/clothing/children/

You first give your audience a name ("Men's Clothing") and then upon choosing the second or third options in the illustration above, you are taken to a new screen where you enter one or more rules based on keywords contained in your URLs. In this case, you would enter "men" as the keyword to define that particular audience. Then, visitors to any page with the word "men" in the URL would qualify. This means that if you also had mystore.com/shopping/shoes/men/, these pages would be included too. If you didn't want this to happen, you could choose the third filter option above and indicate to include "men" but not "shoes". Or, choose the "Custom Combination" option to give you maximum amount of flexibility to include or exclude as many keywords as you want, including and/or combinations. (e.g. Choose men OR women but not children. Or, men AND clothing but not shoes, etc.)

This gives you a quick sense of what's possible, and as you can see, the rules definition allows for both a high degree of flexibility and sophistication when defining your audience, and should even accommodate websites with complex URL structures. (As an aside, if you have yet to create your website or are considering a re-design, you can see how a well-structured layout of your site can be advantageous for both website analytics reporting and retargeting purposes. You should consult your web developer if appropriate changes can be accommodated.)

Website Custom Audiences Usage

As we've stated, one of the key benefits of using custom audiences or website custom audiences is that you are reaching out to visitors, prospects and customers who have already shown interest in your brand or business (vs. general interest and behavior targeting to "cold" traffic). Thus you can re-engage with them in ways that make your ads even more impactful.

Some examples include:

- Target people who have visited your website but have not subscribed to your list

- Target people who have or haven't visited your site within a particular time frame (i.e. last 30-180 days). You can do this to promote new content, or highlight a sale, etc.

- Target people who have reached a particular point in a classic multi-page, time-phased product launch sequence (e.g. Over the course of two weeks, target those who've watched videos 1 & 2, but not 3. Or those who've watched all 3 videos but didn't purchase.)

- Similarly for an ecommerce website, target people who viewed particular products or product categories, or those who reached the order page, but didn't checkout.

- If you have a content-rich website that curates news, articles, videos, etc. across a wide variety of categories and subcategories, you can retarget visitors based on their viewing patterns.

In all of these examples, the purpose of your ads could be to promote new content, updates, discounts, promotions, special offers, and more. Remember, you should never assume why someone did or didn't take a particular action on your site. If someone has shown interest in your products or services but never purchased, or even placed something in the shopping cart but never ordered, perhaps they simply got distracted in the moment — the phone rang, or something else happened that took them away from their computer. It could be for a wide variety of reasons.

Now imagine a day later your "ad" appears in their News Feed that simply invites them to return and complete the purchase.

Done appropriately, these can be extremely effective and result in high conversions. In fact, many marketers consistently find that retargeting produces the highest ROI of any type of ad they run. As you can see, website custom audiences provide very powerful retargeting capabilities that allow you to re-engage, re-market, and "continue the conversation" in ways never possible before.

Chapter 11

Lookalike Audiences

We've just presented a thorough overview of the power and benefits of creating custom audiences and website custom audiences, with one of their primary advantages being that you are targeting people who already have some form of relationship with you. At the very least, they have visited your website and know of you; or, are subscribers who have opted-in to join your email list at some point in time; or, are actual customers and clients who have purchased your products or services.

Within this latter group, you probably also have a subset of dedicated repeat customers who are your greatest raving fans, biggest source of referrals, and who will be loyal customers for life. They love everything about you, your brand, your values, and will support anything you create, produce, and offer. Wouldn't it be wonderful if you could target more people *just like them*?

Now imagine taking these very best customers and doubling, tripling, or even 5x to 10x'ing their size! Imagine taking the very same characteristics, interests, and qualities of your ideal clients and customers, and using those criteria to get many more just like them. Essentially, this is what you try to do manually when targeting new audiences based on demographics, interests, and behaviors. You enter filter criteria based on who you want to attract, and based on the characteristics you *think* your ideal customers have.

But what about the "hidden" traits, interests and likes of your existing audience that you know nothing about? What if there were some common threads woven among the likes and interests of your current (ideal) customer that were completely invisible to you? Perhaps you had no idea that your best clients are big fans of "X", love "Y", and all do "Z" in their spare time.

You may never know, but *Facebook* does! THIS is what Lookalike Audiences can do for you.

Lookalike audiences let you find and reach new people who are likely interested in your business because they are similar to your existing customers, website visitors, or other custom audiences you've defined. Additionally, you can define a lookalike audience based on the fans of your Facebook page, or if you're a mobile app developer, based on users of your existing mobile apps.

Facebook gives you the option to either optimize this audience for similarity (targeting the top 1%) which will be smaller but more precise, or optimize for reach (top 5%) which will be less precise but reach greater numbers. Lookalike audiences can only target one country at a time, but you can create new lists for as many countries as needed. As with custom audiences, you can apply additional targeting to further narrow down as needed, use exclusion targeting, and even target multiple lookalike audiences or combine with other custom audiences within a single ad.

In summary, lookalike audiences is a very effective way to greatly expand your reach, and target a whole new collection of users who are like your existing fans and customers. It removes the guesswork out of how to target more of your ideal audience, by letting Facebook harness all the data it has and do the work for you by putting your message only in front of those who have an affinity and likeness for what you have to offer.

This is the third and final advanced targeting option we discuss in this book, and it's both a fitting end and prime example, once again, of the powerful capabilities and potential that Facebook provides to reach your perfect audience.

Part Three

Chapter 12

Market Research and Audience Insights

In part two of this book, we dove deep into all the selection criteria options for defining your target audience, and we witnessed both the incredible amount of data Facebook provides and the power of utilizing and combining all of this data and criteria to define and reach your ideal market.

An underlying assumption for leveraging these targeting capabilities is that you know the characteristics and criteria of your audience in the first place! In some cases, you might have a strong idea of what these are; in other cases, not so much. Imagine if there was a way to not only have your assumptions confirmed one way or the other, but also receive even more insights and detail about their interests, behaviors, and characteristics. What would it mean to if you could be that much more precise and accurate with understanding your ideal customer and avatar? Imagine how much more financially rewarding it could be if you had a crystal ball to know exactly who your target audience is, and eliminate much of the guesswork for how to find and reach them by leveraging this knowledge. And with that deeper level of understanding, you can further tailor your marketing and messaging even more precisely for greater effect and impact, having that true "message to market match" that can often create huge shifts in results.

The key to these deeper insights and levels of understanding is market research. There are many ways and approaches to do this, including hiring expensive market research firms or paying lots of money for subscription services that provide access to research reports, consumer databases, and the like. However, there are equally powerful free and moderately-priced resources, data sources, and tools you can leverage to conduct your own research, and the payoff for doing so could be huge and well worth your time. This chapter will briefly cover a variety of these tools that can serve as a starting point to launch your own marketing research effort.

If you started this book from the beginning and have read all the way through to this point, you might be wondering, "Wait, you just spent the first two-thirds of this book describing all the data Facebook collects about its users... Can't that be used somehow for research?" And you would be absolutely right! Facebook has one of the largest collections of user data available, and is further enhanced by the third-party data sources it incorporates to provide a variety of other demographic, interests, purchase, and behavior data into the mix. In short, they've taken much of the expensive research data normally only available to those with deep pockets, and have completely integrated it into its own collective pool of information. We'll start with two capabilities available within Facebook itself that will give you incredible insights into your audience profile, and how to best target them.

Facebook Graph Search

At the top of every Facebook page is a search bar, which has always allowed you to search directly for people, pages, groups, and apps on Facebook. Beginning in 2013, Facebook greatly expanded it search capabilities with Graph Search, which now allows you to explore *connections* between people, places, and interests and ask more sophisticated questions that utilize Facebook's entire connected data set. With over 1.3 billion people on Facebook, this results in over one trillion connections.

Graph Search offers an incredible way to discover and explore connections, relationships, shared interests, and things people have in common that may have never been realized before, and is not only fun for individuals to explore their "social graph", but is an incredibly powerful market research tool for gaining greater insights into your target audience. At this time, Graph Search is only available in English for desktop users, and Facebook continues to enhance its capabilities over time.

To use Graph Search, begin typing in keywords or a search phrase. As you type, a list of search suggestions will appear which you can optionally choose. The importance of the search suggestions is that it shows examples of the types of phrases and combinations that can be entered, since there's a syntax (although undocumented) that makes it work. You can search for friends, people, photos, pages, groups, locations, places, and a wide variety of interests that can be combined in multiple ways to get very specific results. To illustrate what's possible, let's provide a few example phrases you can type in:

Friends who live in my city

My friends of friends who live in Chicago, Illinois

People who like surfing and live nearby

Restaurants that my friends like in San Francisco, CA

Music that my friends like

Music liked by people who like music I like

Movies liked by people who like my favorite movies

As you can see just in the examples above, you can tap into any type of interest of your friends, your friends' friends, or people in general and open up a whole new world of discovery. You can combine these with a location and dates (e.g. "Photos of my friends taken in Paris, France in 2014") and any other creative combinations you can think of.

Since there is no definitive list of exactly what search phrases or combinations it will recognize, it is best to just type the general search pattern you are after, and Facebook's suggestions will reveal the proper syntax of the phrase you are trying to string together. If it doesn't provide a suggested phrase, then you need to modify and reword your phrase until Facebook fills in a related suggestion.

With just the initial examples above, you may begin to see how this can be extended to do broader market research. A good place to start is to consider the additional likes and interests of people who like or follow a page related to a brand, celebrity, industry, or market you are going after (and even your competition), or to groups they belong. For example, you can enter

Pages liked by people who like [insert Facebook page]

Favorite interests of people who like [insert interest or page name]

Favorite interests of people who belong to [insert group name]

Do you recall our San Diego fitness gym owner example in chapter 7? Here are three graph search examples I used to identify further interests to target:

Favorite interests of people who are interested in Bodybuilding

Pages liked by people who like Bodybuilding.com and who live in San Diego, California

Magazines liked by people who are interested in Bodybuilding

For another example, let's say you have a B2B business with a particular product or service that caters to dentists or dental offices. After initially targeting dentists and dentistry as a general interest or profession, let's assume you need to further narrow your reach by trying to identify dental practice owners (not just staff), and/or those who are actively involved in professional organizations. You know of the American Dental Association, but what about others? A good place to start is

Pages liked by people who like American Dental Association

What does this reveal? A whole list of pages related to other associations and dental websites like Academy of General Dentistry, American Dental Education Association, California Dental Association, etc. Additionally, you could try

- Groups that people who like American Dental Association joined
- Groups of people who like Dentistry and American Dental Association
- Pages liked by people who like American Academy of Cosmetic Dentistry
- Favorite interests of people who like American Academy of Cosmetic Dentistry

Did you know that a public group named Dental Entrepreneurs exists with over 1700 members, and their focus is on the business side of dentistry? Or a dental news website (dentaltown.com) has over 62,000 followers on their Facebook page, or a World of Dentistry page exists with almost 230,000 fans? Depending on what your focus and purpose is and whom you are trying to target, the results from all of these graph search queries are an excellent starting point for doing a deeper dive.

For the names of Pages and interests, you can target these directly in your audience selection criteria when creating ads. However, since you can't run ads targeting Facebook groups, the best option here is explore the group activities, postings, and membership, and even join the group yourself to participate and build relationships with other members. A lot of insights and revelations may come from active group members over time that could lead you to further targeting ideas down the road. Plus, people who join groups (verses those who just like a page) are often an indicator of more active engagement and stronger interest by those individuals.

Even for non-advertising purposes, joining groups and exploring pages and interests on Facebook related to your profession or industry is an excellent way to benefit your business in other ways. In the process, you may learn about association events, trade shows, hot topics, industry news and trends, and other activities that could serve as additional marketing or sales opportunities for your business down the road. Over time, people will learn about your business too and you can invite them to follow your page. And as your own fan base grows, you can use graph search to learn more about their likes and interests, thus helping you tailor your messaging, add more value, and build stronger relationships with them over time (and advertise to them too!). By joining these groups and actively participating and adding value first, you never know what new relationships will be formed or what new doors of opportunity and growth may open as a result.

In summary, Facebook's graph search is a very powerful tool, and we've just scratched the surface on ways you can use it. There are literally hundreds of possible search combinations that can help you with market research, learn more about your existing fans, and the audiences you are trying to target. Not only are these insights powerful, I know you'll have fun using it!

Facebook Audience Insights

Facebook's most recent tool released in the spring of 2014 is called Audience Insights, and is designed to help marketers learn more about their target audience by providing aggregated information based on a variety of demographics, purchase behavior, page likes, and Facebook usage. The data is viewable based on three segments of people:

- People connected to your page or event
- People in the Custom Audiences you've already created
- The general Facebook audience.

The tool provides insights and trends into your audiences that may not have been visible before, allowing you to tailor your marketing and messaging based on the discoveries you make, as well as use that for new or even more refined targeting than what you were doing before. For example, you may have a Custom Audience based on your existing client or customer list that you've built over the years. Do you have a true understanding of who makes up your clients and customers? Do you know things like what percentage are male vs. female; where they live; their household income; education level; and relationship status? Do you know what their top interests are, and where else they like to spend money? Do you know what other pages they like on Facebook and how active they are on the platform? Now you can!

Audience Insights gives you all of this and more, by aggregating their data into a collective profile and then allowing you to compare your audience make up with the general Facebook populace.

Additionally, you can use the Audiences Insights tool just like the Ad Creation tool, where you can enter various criteria to define your initial audience selection (e.g. Married couples in the US, ages 25-50, with children ages 12 and under). With this base criteria established, you can now view the other demographics, interests, purchase and shopping behaviors, and trends that make up this selection and measure affinity relative to the entire Facebook audience.

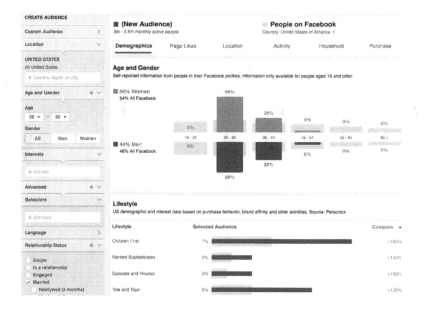

The data is laid out in a nice graphical format spread across six tabs at the top. The charts are also interactive, allowing you to click on a portion to focus on that one segment. You can even turn your Insights data results into a new target audience that you can save directly to your Ads Manager and use for a future ad campaign.

As with all of its tools, Facebook provides these results in an aggregated, anonymous way that maintains people's privacy and never allows individuals to be identified or targeted. Audience Insights is available from your Ads Manager menu, and you should definitely include this in your arsenal of market research tools.

Google

While it may be stating the obvious, Google (or Bing or Yahoo) is an excellent place to do all kinds of research on your market, audience, competition, and more. Going back to our dental example, often times entering general interests like dentists or dentistry in the Facebook ad tool results in a very broad reach (and may consist of many people who express interest in that topic but aren't actual dentists themselves). If you didn't know what to try next, then simply searching for "dental associations" in Google will produce a whole list of results that you can target. Additionally, Google provides a list of suggested related searches at the bottom of each search results page you can try. Search engines are an excellent place to discover organizations, groups, discussion forums, conferences, news and topics, etc. related to your market or industry, and many of the insights gained can be applied back in Facebook when defining your audience selection criteria. Never underestimate what you can uncover with a little sleuthing!

Keyword Research

While keyword research is vital for improving search engine optimization (SEO) and targeting pay per click advertising campaigns in the world of search marketing, it's also essential to understanding the terms, phrases, and language used by your market, customers, and audience as a whole. It reveals the actual words and phrases used and searched for by users, as opposed to the industry-specific jargon and what you *think* they should search for. It can be used as the basis for developing content strategies across your website, social media, and advertising campaigns on Facebook and elsewhere. Additionally, it's an excellent way to keep tabs on and "spy" on your competitors.

Google Adwords Keyword Planner (adwords.google.com/KeywordPlanner), formally replacing their ever-popular Keyword Tool, is still free, but more tightly integrated into the Adwords platform and requires an account to access. While still useful for basic research, there are many other tools as well, including:

- Moz tools (http://www.moz.com/tools)
- Keyword Spy (www.keywordspy.com)
- SpyFu (www.spyfu.com)
- Wordtracker (www.wordtracker.com)
- SEMrush (www.semrush.com)
- WordStream Keyword Tools (www.wordstream.com/free-keyword-tools)

Many of these are paid subscription services, but most of them offer a free trial so you can try them out before committing to a purchase.

Audience Measurement and Analytic tools

If you are looking for other sources of audience measurement data like demographics, affinity, and interest-related data for other websites, along with additional competitive analysis, you can check out these tools:

- SimilarWeb (www.SimilarWeb.com)
- Quantcast (www.quantcast.com)

Of course, don't neglect the insights and analysis you can gain from the visitors to your own website. Be sure to install the free Google Analytics tool (www.google.com/analytics/) in order to analyze your own visitor traffic — where they came from to arrive at your site, what devices they used to get there, how long they stayed and what content they viewed. Combine this with the Website Custom Audience pixel from Facebook for retargeting — and you'll have a more comprehensive picture of your audience's likes and needs, and therefore know what and how to target them again in the future.

Amazon

Amazon is the world's largest bookstore and largest online retailer in the United States, with over $74 Billion in revenue in 2013. One aspect that makes Amazon such a great research tool is that it's essentially a search engine for buyers. People come to Amazon for one primary reason and that's to shop and buy! And that's a good place to be if you want to know what's hot and what "problems" people are looking to solve by virtue of their purchases.

Here are three great tips for using Amazon for research. First, review all the top bestseller books that exist in your industry, market, or niche. Check out the titles, examine the table of contents (using the free "Look Inside" previewer), and see what specific topics and subtopics are being covered. If you find a common theme or repeating subject matter among the top five books, it's likely an important topic people want to know about.

Secondly, look at some of the top reviews for these books, especially those that are marked "most helpful". Why look at reviews? Because revealed here are the very topics, points, content, and material that resonated with the reader, and was important enough to them to call it out in the review. In addition, pay attention to the language, words, and descriptions used by the readers themselves. No matter what the subject is, they are reflecting back on it in *their* words, and this is gold. You can leverage these insights in your future marketing and sales copy, social media posts, blog content, and also for any product, training or course material you may develop in the future.

Finally, at the bottom of every item's sales page is a section entitled, "Customers Who Bought This Item Also Bought" area. This directly shows what other "interests" these people have, and can reveal more clues into the likes and desires of your target market.

Surveys

One of the best ways to learn more about your potential and existing customers is to ask them directly! Using surveys is an excellent way to gather more information about the needs, wants, problems, and challenges your customers and potential customers face, so that you can then align your messaging, content, products, and services to deliver and fulfill on their needs. A good survey, thoughtfully created and properly designed, can yield more insights then perhaps any other data source, and at the same time enhancing and adding to the demographics, psychographics, and other data points you may have already gathered.

The good news is, there are some excellent and very affordable online survey tools you can use to create and conduct surveys. We will mention one here, SurveyMonkey (https://www.surveymonkey.com), but will include other options in our Resources section, available when you sign up for our free book bonuses. Of course, how to properly structure the survey, craft the questions, determine the length, incentivize responses, etc. are all important components to creating and conducting a successful survey. We'll point you to some helpful resources on that too!

Chapter 13
Next Steps

If you've made it this far and have read all the way through from the beginning, congratulations! Or, if you've skipped around and chose selective topics you wanted to learn more about, I hope you found the information and answers you were seeking.

In summary, I hope we achieved our objectives laid out in the opening chapter, and adequately conveyed why it pays to advertise in today's online marketing environment, why Facebook is one of the best advertising platforms to use, and why Facebook's audience selection capabilities are unmatched in their scope, breadth, and depth of targeting.

At the same time, I hope you got inspired and excited about the possibilities this presents for your business! My sincerest wish is that you walk away from this book with a massive amount of value, a collection of new ideas, and the desire to implement this in your business *now*. There is no better platform right now than Facebook to get your products, services, and message out there, and to use paid advertising as the medium to accelerate and maximize your reach to your perfect audience.

Although we've arrived at the end of the journey for this book, the conversation and our relationship together doesn't have to end here! As mentioned many times, we've put together a package of free resources that include checklists, tips, resource guides, future updates to this book, and other unannounced goodies that will assist you on your journey with Facebook.

In addition, we'll keep you current and up-to-date on the latest news in the Facebook and marketing worlds that are directly relevant and useful for your business. Drowning in information already? Let us help you sift through and filter the deluge of news and data, and bring you the very best news you can use.

To access our free book bonus resources, please visit

www.perfectaudiencebook.com/bonus

Or

Text your name and email address to 415-691-BOOK (2665)

Or

Text the word PERFECT to x58885

Or

Scan this QR Code

Additionally, if we can be of any assistance with your Facebook advertising needs or support your other online marketing efforts, we offer consulting, done-with-you and full done-for-you services in a variety of areas. Please visit www.wowcreativemedia.com to review our services and schedule a consultation.

About The Author

Dave Pittman is a two-time #1 bestselling author, an award winning certified consultant, marketing technologist, and entrepreneur.

He is founder and principal consultant at Wow Creative Media, LLC, an online marketing, new media, and business growth consulting company that helps business owners, entrepreneurs, and professionals build their online presence and platform, simplify and automate their marketing, and grow their business. He loves delivering Wow results and a Wow experience for his clients, and helps them discover and unleash their own Wow to promote and accelerate their business growth and profits.

With over 21 years experience in the high tech industry ranging from small startups to global Fortune 100 companies, Dave's breadth of experiences include: consultant, analyst, database architect, web designer and developer, project lead, and marketing intelligence manager of global teams delivering multi-million dollar initiatives. Now, Dave takes his passion for marketing and technology and helps people and businesses leverage these to their strategic advantage for greater benefit, enjoyment, productivity, profit, and growth.

In addition to this book, he is co-author of the #1 International Best Seller "There's Money In This Book: 17 Secrets from a Marketing Mastermind".

Dave resides in beautiful Santa Cruz, CA and loves the ocean, travel, great food and wine.

Footnotes

---

[1]

http://www.businessweek.com/the_thread/techbeat/archives/2007/11/facebook_declar.html

[2]   http://www.allfacebook.com/2q-earnings-15m-advertisers_b133465

[3] https://www.facebook.com/business/news/Organic-Reach-on-Facebook

[4]   http://www.adage.com/article/digital/brands-organic-facebook-reach-crashed-october/292004/

[5]   https://www.facebook.com/business/news/News-Feed-FYI-Showing-More-High-Quality-Content

[6] http://newsroom.fb.com/news/2014/10/facebook-reports-third-quarter-2014-results/

[7] http://techcrunch.com/2014/07/23/facebook-usage-time/

[8] https://www.facebook.com/business/power-of-advertising

[9] Ibid.

[10] Neilson OCR, August 2013

[11] https://www.facebook.com/business/adsguide/?tab0=Mobile%20News%20Feed

Made in the USA
San Bernardino, CA
30 May 2016